SIX-FIGURE
SALARY
NEGOTIATION

INDUSTRY INSIDERS SHOW YOU HOW
TO GET THE MONEY YOU DESERVE

MICHAEL ZWELL, PH.D.

PLATINUM
PRESS®

The Platinum Press® is a registered trademark of F+W Publications, Inc.

Published by Adams Media,
an F+W Publications Company
57 Littlefield Street
Avon, MA 02322
www.adamsmedia.com

ISBN-10: 1-59869-494-4
ISBN-13: 978-1-59869-494-9

Library of Congress Cataloging-in-Publication Data
is available from the publisher.

Printed in Canada.
J I H G F E D C B A

This publication is designed to provide accurate and authoritative information with
regard to the subject matter covered. It is sold with the understanding that the publisher is not engaged in rendering legal, accounting, or other professional advice. If
legal advice or other expert assistance is required, the services of a competent professional person should be sought.

     —From a *Declaration of Principles* jointly adopted by a Committee of the
American Bar Association and a Committee of Publishers and Associations

Many of the designations used by manufacturers and sellers to distinguish their product are claimed as trademarks. Where those designations appear in this book and
Adams Media was aware of a trademark claim, the designations have been printed
with initial capital letters.

This book is available at quantity discounts for bulk purchases.
For information, please call 1-800-289-0963.

To Lori, the love of my life
To Bob Wright, who holds the highest vision of anyone I know

Acknowledgments

My deepest thanks goes to the contributors who coauthored chapters and lent their incredible expertise and wisdom. They are: Catherine Candland, Donald Delves, Mylle Mangum, Stan Smith, Tom Terry, William White, Judith Wright, and Robert Wright.

I also wish to thank the students and faculty at the Wright Leadership Institute who have contributed to my growth and development, with whom I learned and developed many of the key concepts in this book. These include, in addition to many of the names previously listed, Rich Lyons, Brian Laperriere, Jeff Golden, Art Silver, Rob Johnson, Corey Coscioni, Angela Calkins, Jenn Stephen, and many more. The vision and commitment to higher purpose and principles of Bob and Judith Wright, founders of the Wright Institute, has guided my approach to this book.

I also owe this book to all of my employees, clients, and candidates in my twenty-five years of experience at Zwell International, from whom I gained the knowledge and experience to write this book.

This book would not have been possible without Tricia Crisafulli, whose assistance, guidance, and brilliant writing has made this book what it is today. And special thanks to my agent, Doris S. Michaels of the DSM Literary Agency, for her patience and dedication to this book.

Finally, the love of my wife, Lori Jaffe Zwell, my children, Dan and Rachel, my sister, Carol Goertzel, and my father, Leo Zwell, has sustained me throughout.

CONTENTS

The Match Game

You've just learned how to play chess. You understand the rules of the game and basic strategy. Now you're sitting down to a match with a chess master. Do you think you have any chance of winning?

When you enter the job search/salary negotiation process, you're facing the same challenges as the amateur chess player who is up against a professional. You may know the basics of the game, and you may have a strategy. Yet with few exceptions—such as a senior manager who is very experienced with negotiations—most people are grossly outmatched when they are up against a seasoned hiring manager or a human resources professional. It's not that the prospective employer is trying to outsmart you or trick you into taking a job you don't want. Rather, the process is far more complex and convoluted than most people realize.

In chess, there are three parts to the game: the opening, the middle game, and the end game. In the opening, both sides establish their positions. In the middle game, each side develops and takes advantage of his strengths and shores up his weaknesses to develop an advantageous position. In the end game, they go for the close.

In the hiring process, the opening includes finding out about the job, submitting your resume, and the initial interviews. At the end of the opening, you know what the job is, you have interest in the job, and the company has interest in you. The middle game is the continuation of the interview process as each side learns more about the other and discovers the extent to which employer and candidate are a good fit for each other. The end game is the negotiation of a job offer. For most candidates, however, this part of the game is mismatched, pitting an amateur against a professional.

Part of being an amateur is not knowing what strategies and tactics you can use, not understanding the implications of moves that you make, not understanding why your opponent has made the moves he has made, and how to deal with your emotional reactions as you go through the game. Professionals, on the other hand, have a wide repertoire of moves. They instantly see through the tactics of the amateur and can respond immediately to take advantage of the amateur's mistakes and naive assumptions.

Imagine you're an amateur who plays one game of chess every couple of years. Now you're up against a professional who plays chess every day. Good luck. This is the world of salary negotiation in which most candidates live.

In chess one side wins, and the other side loses. In the job world, it's not so simple. Usually, a successful negotiation requires that both sides win. To illustrate, let's switch metaphors. Let's go back in time seventy years to the old-fashioned ritual of courtship and marriage in which the man was always the one who called the woman for a date; the man was always the one who proposed marriage to the woman, and the woman's role was to say yes or no. However, the man did not have all the power. The woman attracted the man and created the situations and circumstances such that he wanted to call her, to date her, and to propose to her. She was the pursued who took responsibility for having the pursuer of her choice catch her!

Unlike the chess game, in the world of courtship, both the man and the woman are after a win/win. Both want a marriage in which they are happy and fulfilled.

This old-fashioned courtship scenario fits today's hiring process. Candidates are the pursued, making themselves as attractive as they can, while at the same time deciding whether they want the offer. Employers are the pursuers, also making themselves attractive and deciding whether they want to go after a particular candidate for a long-term relationship. Even if a candidate takes the initiative to contact a potential employer and says, "I want to work for you," it's still the company's choice to make a job offer or not.

Now, consider the job candidate who has been out of work for a while and fears not being wanted and never getting a proposal. Or consider the candidate who initially receives lots of interest from several potential employers and says, "Oh, I'm so in demand, none of these opportunities are good enough," turns down the initial offers, and ends up with no more. These dynamics all play out in the interview and negotiation process.

In some ways we are much less prepared for the hiring process than we are for courtship. We grow up with books and movies that teach us about the courtship process, and we usually see and experience dating well before we consider a "permanent" relationship. In the hiring process, we confront issues with which we have little experience:

- When asked what salary I am looking for, what should I say?
- What's the salary range in the company for the position that defines the outer limits of what's possible?
- What's the market for the salary for my position, at my experience level, geographic area, etc.?
- What's the culture of the organization, and will I fit in?
- How do I evaluate and compare the benefits package?

- Can I negotiate for more vacation, a flextime arrangement, and company reimbursement for continuing education?
- How can I tell if I'll enjoy working for my manager?
- How can I tell if what they're telling me is true, or are they giving me a line to get me to take the job?
- What is the realistic career path for me if I take the job?
- Does this job fit in with my broader career aspirations?

Not only are we amateurs at addressing these questions, we also need to answer them with limited information about the company and the job and very little time spent with our future manager and others in the company. (Likewise the company has limited information about us.) At most, you've spent several hours together. Think about your last employment review on your job. The assessment made by your supervisor or manager was most likely based on your previous twelve months of work. There was a lot of in-depth data that revealed a fairly complete picture of you, your performance, your strengths, your weaknesses and developmental needs. A hiring manager can't possibly do the same kind of evaluation, even after several interviews.

Through *Six-Figure Salary Negotiation*, you will gain a deeper understanding of what's really going on in the recruitment and negotiation game. You'll learn the questions to ask as you become more discerning and empowered. You'll understand how to value yourself, given your particular job market and expertise, as well as how to manage yourself and your emotions.

Six-Figure Salary Negotiation is loaded with stories of job seekers, recruiters, hiring managers, and top executives, whose real-life experiences will give you in-depth understanding of how the recruitment and negotiation process works. You'll read examples of win/win negotiation in action—as well as disasters in the making.

This book will also provide you with the unique perspective and knowledge from CEOs who are global experts in employment issues.

These top achievers share their insights from both sides of the negotiation table, with techniques and strategies for reaping opportunities, satisfaction, and monetary rewards. Each chapter also includes
self-assessments and other exercises to help you learn more about
your own strengths and weaknesses in the negotiation process, your
priorities for having a work/life balance that really works for you, and
what kind of job would best match your goals, aspirations, and life
journey.

You will understand the biggest mistakes that people make in
their job searches and negotiation. By being aware of these pitfalls,
you can avoid making the same mistakes, or at least recover more
quickly when you do. These mistakes include:

- Not asking the right questions. It's not so much that people lie
  to you, but if you don't ask the right questions, they won't give
  you the information you need.
- Not knowing enough. Most people simply don't have enough
  information and understanding—about the job market, about
  the companies where they are interviewing, about themselves
  and what they really want, about their strengths and weaknesses. . . . When you don't have enough information, you can't
  easily separate fantasy from reality.
- Not thinking sufficiently about your own career path and life
  journey. As a result, you're more apt to make poor choices.
- Not managing your fear and anxiety in ways that maximize
  your opportunities. Ideally you will monitor and use your fear
  to identify areas of concern and issues that you should further explore so that you can make the best-informed decision
  possible.

Through *Six-Figure Salary Negotiation*, you will look more
broadly at the range of elements that make the job search and negotiation process much more than, "How much money am I going to

get?" You will begin asking the essential questions such as: Is this someone for whom I really want to work? What is the career progression from this job? What do I really know about the person in the organization who is hiring me? How can I identify and evaluate the corporate culture?

Many times people are afraid to ask tough questions for fear of being eliminated. My experience is that by asking the right questions and getting the right information you will be far better able to determine if a particular job is right for you. When you avoid taking a job that's not a good fit, you save yourself time, aggravation, stress, emotional upset, and the need to start the search process all over again. Plus, you save the organization from making the mistake of hiring you.

The process of job recruitment and executive placement appeals to me on many different levels—emotionally, intellectually, and as a scholar who has studied human behavior. My own professional history begins when I graduated in 1970 with an anthropology degree from the University of Chicago, where I was a Woodrow Wilson Fellow, and then went on to Yale for my graduate degree. As I was completing my doctorate, I got a job at Rutgers University teaching sociology and anthropology. Sounds like a pretty logical career path, doesn't it?

The problem for me, however, was that this career path was unsatisfying. I had an inkling at this point that I wanted to be out in the world, making a bigger difference, but I didn't know how I was going to get there. All I knew was my current job as a professor wasn't giving me the life experience I wanted.

After academia, I tried my hand at consulting in an area that was known at the time as participative management. I led seminars as a trainer/consultant for corporate clients, then became involved with a company to develop programs to help people change their behaviors around eating and weight loss. Looking back, I can see how this interim phase was moving me in a direction that would use my expertise in human behavior. (I was an anthropologist, after all. Still, I was looking for something else.

Then opportunity knocked. A corporate recruiter whom I met through a mutual connection suggested I go to work for his organization. I started on a Monday, and by the following Tuesday I had made a placement, earning $2,000. This was in 1980, and making $2,000 in one week was very good money. I placed one person my first month, another person the second month, five people in my third month, and I was on my way.

It took me a long time to understand why I was good at placement. I was never someone who liked cold-calling. In fact, if you took at look at who I am—an academic, intellectual person—you'd never put me in a recruiter job. However, at my core I am an anthropologist who loves to understand systems (so much for surface impressions . . .). And I am a good listener and a thinker who is adept at conceptualizing. Plus, I love the deal.

Given my intellectual and personality makeup, I looked at organizations differently than other recruiters. When I took on a search assignment, I looked at the organization holistically—the role of the person within the organization; who the hiring manager is; what makes the organization tick; the culture of the company; what kind of person would excel in that environment; and so forth. I told hiring managers that I couldn't guarantee the first person they saw would be a fit. But I could guarantee that after receiving their feedback based on the interview with that first person, they wouldn't see another candidate from me whom they should not see. In other words, my expertise was in developing an understanding of who they were as an organization and what they needed. I could assess people quickly and identify the fit.

This was great for about five years, but then I got bored. It had lost its challenge for me. I started seeing an executive coach who advised me to bring the best of social science to executive search. That took me on a path that defined my career from then on. From my life and career experience, from my placement of hundreds of people—accountants, salespeople, information technology professionals, engineers, and bankers, and at all levels up to CEOs and board members—I am honored to share my insights with you.

This book is the result of more than twenty-five years in the recruiting field, but it also reflects my passion for research into what predicts performance. I have found, for example, that the key factors that differentiate superior performing individual contributors, regardless of their type of job or career path, are:

- Their ability to influence others
- Their results orientation
- Their initiative

Don't you want to know how you score on all three of these important factors and, more importantly, how you can improve in those areas that are weaknesses and need to be developed?

What research and my experience as a recruiter also told me is that, no matter how good a person is at his or her job, most people lack the skills and mindset to be good negotiators. They can be brilliant, insightful, persuasive, creative, innovative, and all the rest . . . but they still don't know how to negotiate for the next right job. As I said before, this often comes down to not knowing the right questions to ask.

At this point in my life and career, I think of myself as a pretty good negotiator. I've learned to listen to what the other parties really want and need and what really matters to them, and I know that a kep part of my job is to give them what they really want. Making them happy is critical to their giving me what I want: if they are well served, I'll be appropriately and often generously compensated.

For me, negotiating is human-to-human interaction. I like nothing better than having people be deeply satisfied with the work that I do for them, and when I know that they're deeply satisfied, I have no qualms asking for top-dollar compensation for my work. I ask myself how much value can I add, and that leads to the question of how much I am compensated in return. I don't want someone paying me $200,000 unless I'm delivering $400,000 or more in value.

You might be wondering why I'd be satisfied with $200,000 in compensation for twice as much value delivered. Why not $400,000 for $400,000? The answer is there is no reason for someone to hire me if I'm taking out all the value that I'm creating. There is a basic rule of thumb that people's salaries should be one-third of the value they contribute.

My perspective remains consistent, regardless of what side of the table I'm on—whether I'm the employer or the executive. My goal is to make the greatest contribution and to be fairly compensated for that value.

For example, I had a conversation just recently (as this book was being finalized, in fact), with a major client for which I am a subcontractor. At the time we spoke, the executive had been writing a memo questioning whether the firm should launch a new product, because they had recently made an acquisition that took up a huge amount of their resources, including money and attention. He mentioned this to me, and my immediate thought was, how big a role could I play to help solve the client's problem?

So I said to the executive, "I think I can help you." When he asked how, I suggested that I manage the rollout of the new product for all 1,000 of the firm's customers and take complete responsibility for the successful implementation.

Whether or not the transaction gets completed is irrelevant. The point is your job is to maximize your value contribution, make sure that the value contribution is recognized, and negotiate for fair compensation for that value. In order for you to do that successfully you have to know what you can contribute and what you really want.

Even smart, competent professionals often are out of touch with who they are, what they really want, and what is the current state of their industry. They focus on the fantasy of some dream job or inaccurately assess themselves and the job opportunity. They want everything to match up, but they don't see the obvious warning signs and red flags. They walk into the booby traps and sometimes don't even know they've been ensnared in the wrong job until it's too late. This happens more often than you think—even to the most discerning of us.

I remember in my early days as a recruiter when I was doing several senior-level searches for a private bank based in Geneva, Switzerland. For that assignment I spent one week a month for a year in Geneva, a lovely, cosmopolitan city on the shores of beautiful Lac Léman, ringed by the Alps. How bad could that be? Well, after my third trip, I looked forward to a root canal more than going back to Geneva. With all the travel and jetlag, for three weeks out of the month I was exhausted. I would leave Chicago on Sunday afternoon, arrive on Monday morning in Geneva with one hour of sleep, go straight to work and live on espressos to get through the day. I was off-kilter on the time zone all week, until it was time to go back to Chicago—at which point I would have to readjust all over again. When I finally reached some sort of sleep adjustment, it was time to go back to Geneva.

That experience taught me a lot about how different fantasy and reality can be. As difficult as that travel experience was for me, there are professionals out there for whom traveling only one week a month would be a huge improvement on their grueling travel schedules! When I coach people on their next jobs, or even when I advise friends and associates who are contemplating career moves, I use my own experience as an example of how important it is to reality-test our fantasies.

I've made more mistakes than almost anyone else I know. I take risks, I'm a lifelong learner, and I'm a firm believer that life is about learning and growing. Because our job as human beings is to develop and exercise our gifts, we learn much more from experimenting and stretching than staying in our comfort zone. Most of what I've learned has come from taking risks and trying things, the result of which is many successes and many mistakes and failures.

It is my desire that you take the lessons from my own successes and failures, and those from the other CEOs contributing to this book, to build your own career success and satisfaction.

CHAPTER ONE

Finding Your Next Right Job

Dave Jensen had worked in the technology field for his entire career, most recently as a middle manager—that is, until he was downsized as part of massive layoffs at his former employer. After that, Dave engaged in the usual activities of the newly unemployed: networking, sending out resumes, and interviewing. He pursued every job possibility, at least through the first interview. With a month left in his severance package, Dave's job prospects were down to three opportunities.

1. An IT manager in a large, stable company, working in its corporate headquarters. The job prospect was attractive, and Dave especially liked the security of working in the corporate office. One major drawback for him, though, was that he had been told throughout a lengthy interview process—first by a recruiter and then by the hiring manager—that the top salary for the position was $105,000. In his last job, he was making $135,000, plus bonus.

2. Working for a large consulting firm where he would be given a base salary of $125,000 and a chance to earn potentially more from bonuses and other incentives. A major consideration for

Dave was the work/life issue. He was the father of two young sons, and this job would require him to travel all the time. The hiring manager, in fact, told him upfront that he should expect to be on the road from Monday through Friday virtually every week.

3. As a consultant attached to a smaller consulting firm where he would not be an employee but a contractor. There would be some travel involved, although not nearly as much as with the large consulting firm. He would have the potential to make close to $135,000 a year, but as a contractor he would be responsible for paying for his own health insurance, making quarterly tax payments, and funding his retirement plan.

Dave was in quandary about which position would be his next right job, the one he should take. He really liked the idea of maintaining his $135,000 salary level, which made the position with the large consulting firm very attractive, but the more he thought about it, the less he wanted to be on the road every week. Being a consultant/contractor was appealing, but after paying his own benefits and Social Security contribution (as required for self-employed people), he could end up with far less in his pocket. The most attractive job on balance was the IT manager position, which seemed to be the most secure and offered a logical career path. The salary, however, remained a sticking point.

The interview and recruiting process were very involved as Dave pursued the IT manager position. The more he interviewed, the more he liked the job, although he had not reconciled himself with the fact that he would be making $105,000 a year. When he received a surprise call from a senior manager at the company—the hiring manager's boss—Dave was pleased when the executive asked, "How much salary are you looking for?" Dave quickly replied that he wanted to make $150,000. The senior manager took in the information and continued the conversation.

Shortly aferward, the hiring manager called Dave back and questioned the figure he had given her boss. Dave backpedaled and tried to smooth things over by saying he was still very interested in the position. The hiring manager asked if he would accept the offer if it were made to him. Dave replied he would need to see the offer first, but was "very interested." The recruiter later called him to let him know an offer at $105,000 was coming and wanted to know if he was going to accept it. Dave said that he had some questions—including about the benefits package and the job title—but he was certainly leaning that way.

A few days later, the hiring manager made him an offer to become an IT manager at the firm with an annual starting salary of $105,000, plus vacation, health insurance, retirement, and other benefits. Dave reviewed and accepted the offer and started his new job the following Monday—with two weeks left on his severance package.

To review Dave's salary negotiation process, let's look at what did and did not happen.

The Negotiation: What Happened

- Dave was approached by a recruiter who told him from the first conversation what the maximum salary was. Dave replied that the compensation was acceptable, while harboring doubts that he did not express.
- When the hiring manager's boss called him, Dave took that as an opening to ask for more money, which nearly sabotaged the opportunity for him. To salvage the situation, Dave had to give assurances to the recruiter and the hiring manager that he would, indeed, accept the offer with the salary that was first discussed. In all of these conversations, Dave never attempted to understand the company's needs so that he could present himself as a candidate for a job that had more

responsibility and would require his leadership skills and managerial talents.

- At no time did Dave try to negotiate other elements of this compensation package, such as more vacation, educational benefits, and so forth.

What Could Have Happened

- Dave could have done a much more thorough job of learning about the responsibilities, problems, and projects for the IT department, what the critical problems and issues were, and what the leadership needs were to help the department succeed at servicing the organization. Based on this knowledge, he could have presented a broader range of capabilities that he could employ to help the organization achieve its objectives. That could have resulted in him obtaining a higher-level job or being targeted for that job in a near-term promotion.
- Dave could have explored in depth the full benefits available to employees, understood or probed what benefits were negotiable, and negotiated at least for more vacation time and for educational benefits. This would have been worth thousands of dollars to him annually.
- He could have investigated the culture of the organization much more thoroughly, discovering how work gets accomplished, how decisions are made, how teams cooperate (if at all), and so forth. Had he understood how much value he could create, he would have seen that his style fit well with the organization and would have been able to sell himself better.

Perception, Reality, Lies, and Emotion

On the surface, the story of Dave's new job seems pretty straightforward. However, like the saga of any job search and salary negotiation, it is anything but simple. Finding your next right job requires discernment, self-assessment and awareness, emotional intelligence, and the knowledge of how much you don't know throughout this process. Job searches and salary negotiations are rife with emotion, rooted in the reality that how much money a person makes has a direct impact on his feelings of self-worth and self-esteem.

When it comes to negotiating salary, title, responsibility, and other aspects of the job, most people have very little experience. Yet they are up against people who negotiate compensation every day of the week. Even if the hiring manager doesn't, the human resources department does. These people know what they're doing, and most other people don't.

If that weren't enough, the whole recruitment and negotiation process is based upon managing perceptions, projecting the "right" image, and being less than fully truthful. In today's hiring process, both sides try to exaggerate their strengths and minimize their weaknesses.

On one side there is the job seeker, who wants to put the best foot forward, which often means presenting an image and portraying experience and expertise that he believes the prospective employer wants to see. On the other side is the hiring manager, who wants to paint the rosiest picture of the job and the work environment to make it as attractive as possible. In the middle may be a recruiter, whose number one concern is successfully placing a candidate in a job in order to make money and attract repeat business from an employer.

As each says what he thinks the other wants to hear, I can't help but draw the comparison to dating. Courtship and job recruitment are both emotionally charged processes that are geared around attraction. In courtship, you look your best and say the right things. You want to make a good impression to please the other person and hide any flaws that could cause someone to reject you. In the job search and salary negotiation process, people do the same thing, exaggerating their strengths and hiding their weaknesses. If they oversell themselves, they may end up in jobs at which they fail because they did not have the skills and experience to succeed.

You wouldn't think of getting married after a couple of dates. Two people don't have enough information about each other to make such a momentous decision. Yet they make career moves after a few interviews that, while not as long-term as marriage is supposed to be, can turn out to be either tremendously rewarding opportunities to learn and grow as a person—or potentially disastrous. In fact, the odds seem weighted more toward the side of disappointment in job searches because the process does not allow and encourage either party to disclose the truth, the whole truth, and nothing but the truth.

Lynne was aggressively recruited to become a senior-level executive as part of the executive team of a national company. She was happily ensconced in her job as an executive of a regional operation for another large company when a headhunter contacted her. She was attracted by the picture that he presented to her of being part of the leadership team. She was especially interested in the opportunity to develop employee-training programs and to be the liaison to the company's philanthropic foundation. Through three rounds of interviews with board members, Lynne thought she asked discerning questions about her responsibilities and the goals of the corporation. Based on what she was told, she accepted the position.

Once she was on the job, however, she discovered that the responsibilities of her position were entirely different from what she had been told. After a few months she asked why she had not been told the truth about her job responsibilities and the problems that the company was having—including in-fighting on the executive team. The board member replied, "If you knew the truth about the job, we didn't think you would have taken it."

They were right; Lynne wouldn't have. Now, having been in the job for less than a year, she has prepared her resume and is already in the market for a position that more closely matches her career needs and wants.

I'd like to say that Lynne's experience is an unfortunate anomaly. Sadly, it happens more often than people think. Job titles that have been promised don't materialize. Responsibilities change, or other tasks—including ones that might have been delegated in the past to support staff—bog the job down. The picture of the harmonious work environment turns out to have been grossly distorted. Even the pay that was promised—as in you'll be making "X" in six months—is never delivered.

Why does this happen? The job recruitment and negotiation process is booby-trapped with misleading or limited information on both sides, plus perceptions and fantasies that cloud judgment and distort reality. Although the company says it's in a robust and growing environment with new opportunities on the horizon, it could be going through all sorts of inner turmoil or corporate restructuring, facing economic realities from narrowing profit margins to new competitors in key markets. The job seeker may have a gap, blip, or some other kind of incongruity in his employment history, or she may be taking a big step down in salary because she was overpaid in her last position. It all needs to be managed, massaged, and explained.

To top it all off, there are the job seeker's own emotional swings from the scarcity mindset ("My severance package/savings account/ patience . . . is running out, and I better take any job") to false euphoria ("I'm better than anyone else in this field, and I'm not taking a dime less than my salary objective, no matter how grossly inflated and out of line with current market conditions it is.")

My goal in this book is to help people become better job seekers and salary negotiators by becoming more successful at uncovering and avoiding those traps that can lead them down the wrong career path to an unsuitable job, cause them to pass over better opportunities, or sabotage their own success. The objective is to help you become more informed and empowered throughout what can be a stressful and emotionally difficult process. The key is to know how to ask the right questions, to listen with more discernment to the answers given, and to rein in your emotions to make more logical, objective decisions.

Anyone who thinks that job recruitment and salary negotiation is *just* about money, or is a game in which one side tries to win at the expense of the other, is sorely mistaken. It is about creating a winning solution, which includes a compensation package with base salary, bonus, and other incentives. The process is comprehensive and holistic, and it starts with a job seeker.

IT'S ALL ABOUT YOUR CONTRIBUTION

THE TRAP: You think that maximizing your income is the ultimate win.

THE LESSON: I saw a cartoon many years ago in which an interviewer is sitting across the table from the candidate, telling the person that he is unqualified, doesn't have enough experience, wasn't successful enough in previous jobs, and doesn't dress well. The candidate's reply: "You haven't talked about benefits."

I have interviewed thousands of candidates who, not unlike the one in the cartoon, were focused solely on what was in it for them—to the point that I doubted whether they even heard what I was saying about the job. All that mattered to them was how much they were going to be paid.

THE TIP: Focus on how much you can contribute to the company, not on how much you're going to get out of it.

As a recruiter who has placed hundreds of people—individual contributors to managers to CEOs and directors of boards—and as an entrepreneur who has personally hired dozens of people, I know this process well. The best advice I can give to job seekers is to understand that salary negotiation is different from any other business deal you've been involved in. Unlike most transactions in which the buyer wants to buy as low as possible and the seller wants to sell as high as possible, salary negotiation must be based on an equilibrium of fair value for both sides.

Employers don't want to overpay for someone, nor should they. That would be unhealthy for both sides. Savvy employers also understand that they don't want to underpay either. An employee who doesn't make enough money won't feel valued and will become resentful, undermining morale and motivation. Most experienced managers and human resources departments understand that salary negotiation must be a win/win arrangement if there are to be happy, productive employees with pay packages that are going to work and satisfied employers who believe that they are getting their money's worth.

With that understanding, let's take a second look at Dave's story to discover the traps, clouded perceptions, and emotional issues involved.

The Negotiation Game

From the first conversation with the recruiter, Dave was very interested in the IT manager job with the large company. He liked the idea of working in the corporate headquarters, which was a short commute from his home. The salary, however, was an issue. The recruiter explicitly told him in the beginning that the top salary for the position was $105,000. The only number Dave had in his mind, however, was the $135,000 he had made in his last job.

Dave's feelings are understandable. Like it or not, we live in a society in which self-worth is largely defined by how much money a person makes. We can deny it, but for most of us, social status is linked to income. Therefore, accepting a reduction in pay or getting a smaller raise than someone else is a direct hit to our self-esteem. Think of professional athletes who are making millions—even tens of millions—yet they complain that they aren't getting paid as much as some other superstar. In the corporate arena, especially in the days of stock option mania, corporate executives who receive compensation packages amounting to a hefty seven-figure total feel they need to keep up with their CEO peers who are making eight figures! Their own emotionally charged perception is that they are on a lower rung of the ladder because their pay is less.

The same holds true for the rest of us. Dave liked the fact that in his previous job he made a six-figure income by a comfortable margin. If he took the job with the large company, he'd be just a few thousand over that line. He wasn't basing this decision on the fact that the market had changed. Corporate downsizing in recent years meant there were more middle managers in the technology market than before. He was the same person he was before, with the same strengths and weaknesses. Yet he felt differently about himself making $105,000 versus $135,000.

Job seekers need to understand that what to them is a reflection of their self-worth is just a financial number to an employer. From the company's perspective, it's just part of doing business; employers need to pay a certain amount to get a job done. Companies understand that salaries are necessary costs of doing business. If an employer pays more than a job is worth, it affects everyone else. The pay scale becomes skewed and, while salary is normally a confidential issue, even the suspicion that someone is making more than everyone else in the same job or at the same level can hurt morale.

Many Factors Influence the Job Market

When Dave was making $135,000 a year, he was being overpaid. He might not want to admit that to anyone—maybe not even to himself. But when his former employer hired him, the market for information technology (IT) professionals was tight, and as a result salaries were high.

I remember a conversation I had in 1999 with the head of human resources for a large video game company. When I asked what type of competency assessments they used as part of their hiring process, the HR director told me, "If people walk in the door and say they know JAVA (a computer programming language), we hire them."

In the boom days of the Internet, programmers were a hot commodity and could virtually name their price. Today, it's a much more balanced and rational job market.

Never Turn Down Anything Initially

Even though Dave was put off by the top salary for the IT manager job, he pursued it. This is a cardinal rule in finding the next right job: Never turn down anything initially. Consider every job possibility. If nothing else, you will have more interviewing experience and gain insight into what type of job and work environment would suit you best. Your interactions may lead to all kinds of opportunities that you never would have had if you had cut off discussions at the beginning.

In fact, that's how Dave ended up pursing one of his final three job prospects. A friend of his had recommended him for a position at a small company. From the beginning, Dave suspected that the job was more of an entry-level position, but he still went for the interview. For one thing, Dave knew that small companies have much more discretion and latitude with job titles and responsibilities and, as a result, with compensation.

At the interview, the manager quickly surmised that Dave was overqualified for the position. Their meeting turned into a very engaging and enjoyable discussion about the technology field and what was happening in their industry. At the end of their meeting, the manager gave Dave the name of someone at a large consulting firm that was looking for experienced professionals.

What Looks Like a Great Job Can Be Bad for You

Dave called the person at the large consulting firm and was brought in for an interview. He knew from an acquaintance who worked there that although he'd be a technology consultant, this was not your typical Internet shop where jeans and T-shirts were the corporate uniform. This was first and foremost a consulting firm that offered a variety of services to high-level corporate clientele. Dave got out his best suit and tie.

Dave knew from his career coach that every juncture in the job search process—from the first conversation with a recruiter or human resources person who makes the initial call through all the subsequent interviews—is part of the negotiation process. How he dressed, his verbal and nonverbal communication, even his handshake reflected his confidence, competence, and sense of self-worth and therefore played a part in negotiation.

Meeting with a manager at the consulting firm, Dave heard the right number: the salary was in line with the $135,000 he had been making—plus with bonuses and other incentives it could very well be closer to $150,000. Dave was hooked.

The problem is, when a company is dangling a lucrative offer and all you can think about are the dollar signs, you may be blind to the bigger issues of what your job really entails. Will you be happy? Does this job make sense for you at this stage of your life? Will your personal/family life suffer?

What Dave failed to take into consideration at first was the travel demands. The job required that he be on the road Monday through Friday. He would be offsite, at a client operation, for months on end. He might be in Kalamazoo every week for four months, then in Miami every week for six months. Dave certainly hadn't forgotten that he had a wife and two young sons whom he loved very much; he just temporarily convinced himself that he could "make it work."

When Dave spoke to me about it, I reminded him about our mutual friend, Rick, who graduated with an MBA in 1991 and was immediately offered a job with a major consulting firm that would pay him—at the age of twenty-six with virtually no real-world job experience—a very lucrative salary (especially at the time) of $70,000 a year plus bonus. As Rick's advisor explained to him at the time, it was a lot of money but a wrong career move.

By becoming a consultant at that stage of his career—a twenty-something with an engineering undergraduate degree and a freshly minted MBA—he would not build the kind of substance experience-wise that would serve him in the long-term. He would be traveling all the time, which would also take a heavy toll on him personally—including his marriage. Rick listened to his advisor, turned down the job with the big salary, and took a position with a small manufacturing firm that paid him $20,000 less. This career move launched him on a tremendous learning curve in every aspect of how the business operated. From there he moved into a sales position with a growing IT consulting firm and, several years later, started his own IT consulting firm. Had he followed the other scenario and become a high-paid consultant right out of graduate school, Rick believes he never would have had the same rewarding career and the strong family life with his wife and two daughters that he now enjoys.

Most people fail to realize the implications of what they are negotiating today. They are fixated on salary or job title. They don't realize that the job offer they entertain today will determine their future. Take Janet, who recently became the head of human resources for a growing company in the health care field. The job is exciting and very well paid, giving her the opportunity to learn, grow, and make a difference. In many respects, she is the right-hand person to the CEO. Sounds great, right?

Well it is, except for the one thing that Janet didn't take into consideration when she negotiated the job offer. She spent the first six months traveling five days a week—every week. Single with no children,

Janet didn't think this would be a major issue for her. But after the first few months the wear and tear of constant travel was becoming a huge burden. She was rarely home, couldn't keep up with her friends and the hobbies she enjoyed, and when she was back in her condo all she did was prepare for the next trip. She stopped exercising, and eating meals out with executives and managers led to a fifteen-pound weight gain, which made her feel less energetic and healthy. Janet loved her job, but she hated the toll it had taken.

Fortunately, Janet was able to renegotiate her job demands after six months, changing her schedule so that she traveled every other week, giving her more time at home. It took a lot of effort to accomplish that change, and it affects how she does her job; however, she is committed to making it work for herself and the company.

Dave listened to these stories, and he finally agreed. The IT manager job at the large firm, on balance, was a better prospect. He wasn't closing any doors, however, including when a contractor/consultant position at a small firm materialized.

Know What You're Really Negotiating

The small consulting company would not require the heavy travel that the larger firm would, which was a plus in Dave's book. The idea of being a contractor and not an employee was a wrinkle that he hadn't anticipated, but he liked the bottom-line number of $135,000. Beyond all that, however, there was another issue. He didn't feel entirely comfortable with the manager for whom he'd be working.

The manager was polite and friendly enough at first, but he had habits that Dave found annoying. For example, during their interview, he took no less than four phone calls—none of them urgent, from the sound of it—and never apologized for the interruption. While Dave was talking, the manager's attention was constantly diverted to whatever was on his screen.

By the time we talked, however, Dave had already begun to minimize this, saying the manager was probably very busy, and like most techies he probably was absorbed in his e-mails. My advice was to pay close attention to that red flag.

The first question to consider when you enter into salary negotiation is, What am I negotiating? The answer is, You are negotiating your relationship with your boss, as well as your salary. You are negotiating what your path is going to be in the organization. You are negotiating the next stage of your life path.

This may sound anathema in a salary negotiation book, but money is nowhere near the most important thing. Yes, employees need to feel valued and be fairly compensated and given the opportunity to be well rewarded when they greatly exceed performance expectations. But the wrong job with a great salary is still the wrong job. According to research, it's bad for everyone involved.

The *Gallup Management Journal* survey reported that "happy employees are better able to handle workplace relationships, stress, and change," which can also contribute to greater productivity. Gallup also found that one of the biggest contributors to employee engagement on the job was "a positive relationship with the supervisor."

Thus, the kind of relationship you're going to have with your boss is at least as important in determining job satisfaction as the size of your paycheck and bonus.

Traps, Lessons, & Tips

DO YOUR HOMEWORK

THE TRAP: You get the title, compensation, and responsibilities on paper, but you've been living in denial about what the job really entails and the situation the company is really in.

THE LESSON: Scenario Number 1—You get the right job, right title, and the right money at a company, and ninety days after you start working there it files for bankruptcy. (And, yes, I know people to whom this has happened.)

Scenario Number 2—You get the right job, right title, and right money on paper. You go to work at the new company only to discover that you were misled about what the job really entails and what the organization is really like. It takes you two years to get yourself another job that is more suited to what you want.

THE TIP: Exhaustively ask questions and do your homework. (And read the rest of this book.)

After a second interview with the manager, who seemed just as distracted and hard to communicate with, Dave was far less interested in the small consulting firm. The fact that the $135,000 figure he had been told now seemed less certain also made the position far less appealing.

Meanwhile, discussions with the large company continued with a second and third round of interviews. Dave was also asked to design and deliver a PowerPoint presentation, which he did with some help. This made him wonder what kind of support he would receive at the company, something he'd need to address in his negotiations.

Is It True or Only What They're Telling Me?

Throughout his discussions with the large company, Dave wondered if the salary cap for the IT manager's job was really $105,000—or were they only trying to hire him "on the cheap" because they knew he had been laid off. After all, he had been told that companies do not always give all the facts—just as job candidates sometimes present themselves in a less-than-candid way.

Think about the ever-popular question asked by interviewers: "What would you say is your biggest weakness?" You can't possibly admit, for example, that you need development in presentation skills, or that you need to improve your ability to close sales, even though that may be the truth. You can't say that you need to be better organized and manage your time more efficiently, although you're well aware of that need. By the way, in the typical interview process, there are only a couple of acceptable answers to this question:

1. I'm really bad at work/life balance—I just work too much!
2. I'm too impatient with people who aren't as committed or competent as I am.

(I've been known to ask people the weakness question and then say, "The two acceptable answers to this question are that 'I just work too hard' or that 'I am impatient with others.' So instead of giving me one of those answers, tell me about your *real* weaknesses.")

Many companies claim to have cultures that support the development of their employees, encouraging them to learn and grow. This is absolutely at odds with the typical interview process, in which candidates deny or hide all their weaknesses and exaggerate their skills and expertise and companies present the most optimistic scenarios. This propensity to color the truth leaves both sides suspicious. That's exactly what happened to Dave.

Now remember the part in Dave's story when the senior manager—the hiring manager's boss—called him. Among the things the senior manager said was, "I understand that you're a very good candidate. How much salary are you looking for?"

Dave replied that he was looking for $150,000, based on his last salary and the expectation of getting an increase. The senior manager seemed to take it all in stride.

Major red flag! Dave had fallen into a trap without even realizing it, and he was in serious jeopardy of not being offered the job for which he was a final candidate. He didn't comprehend the extent of the damage that he had done until the hiring manager called him soon thereafter. "Why did you tell my boss that you wanted $150,000? We wouldn't have interviewed you if we had known that! I told the recruiter from the beginning that the salary wouldn't be more than $105,000."

All Dave could do is assure the hiring manager that he was "very interested" in the job. When she asked him what salary he would accept, Dave did try one more time to see how much might be available. "Make me your best offer," Dave replied.

"I'm not going to make you an offer that you're not going to take," the hiring manager told him.

When Dave called me for advice, I explained to him the seriousness of the situation. He might have jeopardized his chances by throwing out a much higher salary figure. The employer was now wondering if he would take the job offer with the $105,000 salary and whether he would be happy and stay. Recruitment and retention are costly considerations for employers. If they think a job prospect is only acting out of desperation, they will probably hesitate to hire that person. Most companies are looking for long-term employees, particularly in a job such as the one Dave was seeking. They don't want to hire someone who is going to be unhappy and leave.

In the end, Dave was able to reassure the hiring manager and the recruiter that he was very interested in the job. When the offer was made at $105,000, he accepted it. For Dave, the new job offers a competitive salary—although not as high a number as he wanted—along with a good benefits and retirement plan that increase the total value of his compensation package. More importantly, he's in a corporate culture in which he feels comfortable, working with a boss he likes, and doing a job that will challenge him and lead to new opportunities to learn and grow.

He has found his next right job.

It's always a good idea to get advice and counsel from an expert in salary negotiation. Having someone on your side who understands the complexities of the process will help you sort through the issues and develop your strategy and tactics to get the result you want.

We all have blind spots, emotional issues, and concerns that deserve to be talked through and clarified, first in our own minds. A coach can be very helpful in this process. Once we have clarified our issues, concerns, and desires, we're ready to negotiate with our prospective employer.

In Dave's case, without coaching he might not have received the job offer. It is likely that the company would have been too apprehensive about the decrease in salary to see him as a viable, long-term employee. Coaching helped him communicate serious interest throughout the interview process to the company while at the same time resolving his feelings about taking a 22 percent salary reduction. In the end, he worked through his personal issues and accepted the job wholeheartedly.

The Best Start

Finding your next right job means starting the right way. From the moment you begin the interview process, you have engaged in the process that will not only determine your salary, benefits, and other elements of your employment package, but will also influence your career path to future opportunities. To do this most effectively, you need to ask the right questions and gather the information you need.

Without adequate information, it will be impossible for you to separate fantasy and your image of the "dream job" from the reality of what is really being offered to you. You won't think about a job beyond the immediate opportunity in order to consider sufficiently your career path and life journey. And you won't manage your fear and anxiety in ways that will maximize your opportunity. In the end, you may think that you've negotiated a good deal because you get a little extra money or a few more days of vacation the first year, but you haven't looked broadly at enough elements that help you decide if this is really the job you want.

To negotiate successfully you need to know how the game works. By the time you reach the end of this book, you will be prepared to play fairly with the intent that you and your future employer will reach a mutually satisfying win/win arrangement. You'll know what to look for and what questions to ask; you'll avoid the traps and the red flags—including the ones you might set off. You'll come to understand your own value as well as the current dynamics of your job market.

As a result, you'll end up not only with a job but the right job that represents the next step on your life path, one that challenges you to build on your current foundation of skills, experiences, and capabilities and that moves you forward in your life journey as you serve the larger community. I believe that the mission for each of us is to use our gifts and talents to fulfill ourselves and contribute to the world as we do so.

Finding your next job will be a process of self-discovery and will make your journey even more of an adventure.

JOB SEEKER'S SELF-ASSESSMENT

The job recruitment and salary negotiation process is as complex as a game of chess. The problem for most people, however, is that they're only amateur players, and they may be up against a real champion—especially when they deal with HR. To be your most effective, you need to be aware of your strengths as well as your weaknesses. It's far better to know now where you will likely shine as well as where you need help or coaching before you're in the midst of negotiation with your next potential hiring manager.

The purpose of this exercise is to help you determine your skills and competencies as you begin the job search and salary negotiation process. In this exercise, you will rate yourself on a scale of 1 to 5, with 1 being "lowest level of expertise," and 5 being "highest level of expertise." Afterward, we'll discuss your scoring.

_____ Negotiating win/win solutions
_____ Doing a market analysis for my position based on my experience and compensation level
_____ Identifying what work I'm passionate about
_____ Identifying the strengths and weaknesses of my potential manager through the interview process
_____ Identifying and evaluating the culture of the prospective new employer and how well I fit in that culture
_____ Identifying what's important to me in a job
_____ Evaluating the economic value of a benefits package
_____ Identifying the potential causes of dissatisfaction in the future position
_____ Envisioning the logical career path from this position
_____ Evaluating my competencies, strengths, and weaknesses that will determine my success in my job
_____ Evaluating if the job is right for me
_____ **Total**

SCORING

Your Score	Your Assessment
45 or More	You are ready for battle.
34 to 44	I hope you're up against an inexperienced employer; otherwise you'll need coaching.
24 to 33	You definitely need coaching.
Below 24	You're fish food!

CHAPTER TWO

What Is Your Value?

with Stan Smith

Searching for the next right job means finding an opportunity that maximizes the value to you and maximizes your value to the organization. Most people associate value with money—a price tag, if you will. Value, however, can be derived in all kinds of ways, some of which can be quantified in dollars and others that cannot. Moreover, what you find valuable someone else may not and vice versa. As part of your search for the next right job, it's important to look beyond salary alone and examine the other aspects of the offer.

In looking at the total value of an offer—including such things as the training you will receive, your opportunity to mentor others, and amount of direct influence you'll have with customers and vendors—you will see a fuller picture of the job that you're considering. When weighing two different offers based upon those factors that are the most valuable *to you*, one job may be far more attractive than the other, even if the salaries are the same.

At the same time, you must also know your own value as you engage in the job offer negotiation process. Being aware of your unique strengths and abilities, as well as those areas in which you are in need of further development, will help you pick the job that is the best match for where you are right now. Knowing what you bring to a job and what you need to be satisfied will give you a better chance of finding a position from which you can derive enjoyment, feel challenged and motivated, and make a positive contribution to those around you. By knowing and appreciating your own value, you will have a more successful negotiation.

During his job search and negotiation process, Dave Jensen admits, he never thought much about the concept of "value." He did not engage in any discussions with the company around such topics as career development and future opportunities. Instead he kept his questions focused on the day-to-day demands of the current job. Looking back, Dave sees he kept his questions to a minimum because he was worried about asking the wrong questions.

While Dave is happy with his new employer and sees a promising future ahead, he admits that his reticence to explore the value proposition limited his ability to articulate his value to the new employer. Instead, he was operating on the basis of limited information. Now, having been on the job for six months, Dave appreciates how his job fits into a much broader IT corporate initiative. "Had I known that, I would have been better able to show how I could contribute," he says. "I would have been able to find out more about the project ahead of time, which would have enabled me to hit the ground running. Who knows? I might have even gone for a higher-level position, if one was available, because I would have seen how my experience and knowledge are aligned with what the company is doing. But I never engaged in those discussions."

Had Dave only known, he would have focused his discussions with his hiring manager around the topic of value. Unfortunately, he did not have the vision and the courage to do so.

In this chapter, Stan Smith, Ph.D., the world's foremost authority on the value of life and "hedonic damages" (meaning the loss of the enjoyment of life), shares his insights into how we derive value from our life and work. He received his doctorate in economics from the

University of Chicago and is the founder and CEO of Smith Economics Group, Ltd. Through his business he is engaged primarily in evaluating damages for commercial and personal injury cases, including loss of job. His work with attorneys and their clients over the years offers fascinating insights into how people value their work, aspects of their employment that they value even more than salary, and the value that they bring to their work.

• • •

When you talk about work, what are the components of value? Is it strictly pay, or are there other elements?

The value of work is not just salary—the present earnings capacity—but also the satisfaction that you get in your employment that goes beyond what you are paid. I have interviewed hundreds of people who have been injured, and almost all of them say that they would rather go to work and face all the challenges that go with that than sit home and collect the same amount of money.

Our well-being is not just associated with making more money or accumulating more assets. That type of thinking reflects the notion that humans are really "Homo Economicus," rational beings who always make decisions that maximize profits. But we are not rational when it comes to these decisions. We are emotional, and we make choices that are largely unconscious.

• • •

So one goal for someone in the job negotiation process would be to become more conscious, to undertake the self-reflection and introspection necessary to know what she truly wants— and not just accept what she thinks she wants or what others have.

Exactly. Here's an example of that. According to classic choice theory, the more options a person has the better. But that's not the way it is for most people. If a person is on a diet, for example, and you give him too many choices—some of which are fattening and do not offer good nutritional value—that would actually be a negative. On the face of it, we may think we want as many choices as possible, but the reality of it is that we would rather limit our choices.

•　　•　　•

So by becoming more conscious about our careers, we see that work is more than a means to make money. We understand that work, in and of itself, is valuable to us. We derive meaning from what we do, the impact we make, the opportunity to make a contribution, and from the challenges and even the failures that allow us to learn and grow.

There are many ways to derive satisfaction from our work that have nothing to do with the money we earn. One aspect is the relationship with colleagues—not just the collegiality of it but also the challenge to learn and to grow by being managed by others and by being a manager of others. Another consideration is the opportunity to learn and improve skills and technical levels. We derive satisfaction from being pushed to the cutting edge of our job in developing skills. We also find satisfaction when we have a positive impact on customers and the marketplace.

Another thing to consider is that we want challenges. We don't want a flat experience. Psychologists tell us that we store experiences based on the peak and the finish. If the peak has a positive value and/ or it ends well, then we think of that experience as having a positive value. The implication for your career is to have jobs that provide peak experiences. People are going to be happier and will derive more value from a job that has highs—as well as lows—than a job that is steady and doesn't vary much.

• • •

Staying in this philosophical vein for now, let's take a look at the issue of comfort. Think about the phrases we use every day. Let's say two people meet for lunch but now it's time to go back to their respective jobs. What do people say? "Don't work too hard." Or, "Take it easy." Think about that for a minute. What those phrases literally mean is "Don't engage, don't strive to do your best."

Taken literally, those phrases mean "Have flat, comfortable experiences in your job." But most people don't want that. People whose jobs are little more than paper-processing with no change usually report that they hate their jobs. Why? Because it is the same day in and day out, without peak experiences—positive and negative.

So using our example of two people saying goodbye and returning to work, what they should be saying to each other is, "I hope you have difficulties and challenges today and problems to address that will allow your talents to be revealed!" We should love the difficulties that give us the chance to rise and shine.

• • •

On a practical level, let's address those professionals and middle managers who are making a six-figure salary. What are some common value drivers for them?

These are precisely the people who have a broad spectrum of work relationships with bosses and colleagues. They experience the opportunity, the satisfaction, and the challenge of rising through the company—and of bringing up and mentoring other people. They have the opportunity to address the issue of value in all its dimensions. In addition to financial compensation, this includes mentorship, leadership, skill development, challenge, opportunity, and so on.

KNOW WHAT YOU VALUE AS YOU NEGOTIATE

THE TRAP: Focusing on money and not on all that is valuable to you.

THE LESSON: Mary left the job where she was part of a successful team, gained new skills, learned more about her field, was mentored by a senior executive, and mentored others. It was only after she moved to a position at a different company that required her to work remotely from her home that she realized how important those aspects of her job were. She missed operating as part of a team, learning and growing, contributing to others, and so on, and had never realized how valuable those things were to her.

THE TIP: Comprehensively inventory what you value, and evaluate opportunities based on that full inventory.

In the job offer negotiation process, how would someone find out about the opportunity to be mentored and to mentor others?

One way would be to interview other people in the organization— people who aren't making the decision about your employment. Ask for the chance to speak with other employees. Or, you may know other people who work for the company. Ask them what their opportunities are to mentor others and to be mentored. This is important information to find out about a company's culture from people within the organization.

• • •

Among the important things to look at when evaluating negotiating a job offer, in addition to salary, would be: what will I learn; who will I work with; and how will I be engaged in the job?

Yes, you want to know not only to whom you'll report but also whom you will be responsible for. People love to volunteer and mentor others. America is the most volunteering nation on the planet and the most charitable per capita—even when it comes to such things as giving blood, which you can do whether you're rich or poor. We have a tradition of giving and mentoring in this country that extends to work. We like to help others grow and learn. The more you can do that in a job, the greater your satisfaction.

Another consideration is to look upward in the ranks above you. We all want the opportunity to be mentored, educated, and coached. We want to increase our opportunities to learn and grow. Having a respected and competent boss is a high value. In fact, the opportunity to be coached and mentored is an important value-driver, independent of salary.

• • •

These factors—the opportunity to be mentored and to mentor others, to make a tangible contribution—could make a big difference between two jobs that, based on salary and job responsibilities alone, look pretty similar. In other words, someone may be looking at a job that appears to be a lateral move

because she would be doing similar things and receiving a similar amount of pay. But when you look at these other factors, it may not be a lateral move at all.

One job may have a huge increase in value when it comes to giving to others and being mentored and tutored. Some of the intangible aspects of a job are the relationships that allow you to grow and learn, relationships that you have with people inside the company and outside the company with clients, vendors, and even the public at large.

•   •   •

Of course, nobody is going to pay someone $100,000 or $150,000 a year to lick envelopes. You're expected to make a meaningful contribution to the organization. People are expected to commit significant energy and resources to their jobs. At the same time, there is a big value to be derived by the individual from that engagement. Yet there is risk in full engagement. What you do becomes more important. Succeeding matters more. Failures hurt more.

The element of risk plays a role in everything. Every time people try to do something they have not done before, they are taking a risk. Most people like some element of risk—there is little learning or growth without it. Everyone's definition of risk is different. For one person it could mean speaking up in a meeting or expressing an opinion. It might be getting to the next level of assertion in a group. It could be taking on a challenging assignment knowing that you might not succeed.

• • •

When looking at the value of two jobs, I have to evaluate them on the basis of how challenged I'm going to be. Let's say one job is easy; I can do it in my sleep. Then there is this other one where I have to learn and grow and take a risk. There are some aspects of this second job that I don't know. There are different values that can be assigned to those two situations.

Ultimately, people report greater satisfaction when they have more challenge and are able to meet it. When we read about people who challenge themselves in sports, business, or some other field, we read it with respect. But with regard to our own careers, we tend to focus on our annual rate of pay as the most important variable of all. If we look at all the other intangible aspects of the job, however, we will find that they provide satisfaction that is more important than a few extra dollars in our pension funds.

• • •

Thinking about my own experiences, I have received tremendous value by doing something that I haven't done before—no matter the outcome. Even if you try something and you don't succeed, the wisdom and experience that you gain will help you do other things in the future. These are benefits that you can't quantify with salary.

These are aspects of the job that are extremely important and independent of the salary itself. For example, it is important to me to have the highest positive impact I can have. If I am considering two jobs with the same salary, I would want the job where I perceive that I can make the most contribution to my boss, to my clients, and to others. I want to work where I can achieve or accomplish the most. It really isn't just about the money.

• • •

But isn't the standard thinking for most people, "If I make more money I'll be happier?" Are you saying that this isn't true?

When it comes to money and happiness, it's all relative—literally. Numerous studies have shown that most people feel happier in an $80,000-a-year job where they are making more than the majority of other people at the company than they would in a $100,000 job where they are earning significantly less than other people. Similarly, people feel better about their house when it's the nicest one on the block than if it's the same house but it's the worst one on the block. So if you're going to earn $125,000, you'd be better off—in terms of your happiness—in a place where your colleagues are earning slightly less than you are instead of the other way around. Bottom line: We do compare ourselves to other people.

• • •

This may not make the most sense, however, for salary growth in the future. If you're one of the top-paid people in the company or in a particular job category, you may not have room to grow. You may have to advance to another level, become a manager, or even leave the company in order to earn significantly more.

Yes, but we still need to be aware that we rank ourselves and compare ourselves to other people. It is what people do. As I said before, we think we make rational decisions, but we do not. We say that we make decisions that make us happier, but we do not. So if people have the choice between two jobs—one that pays $80,000 but they're among the highest paid, and one that pays $100,000 but they're among the lowest paid—then other things being equal, people take the $100,000 job. Research shows, however, that people in the $100,000 job where they are the lowest paid will have a greater chance of feeling unhappy and unsatisfied, which is the exact opposite of their goal to be happy. From that standpoint alone, they would be better off with the $80,000-a-year job—even though that might not make sense from a long-term financial standpoint.

• • •

That's a real eye-opener for most people—what's rational, what's irrational, what makes them happy, and what may lead to discontent even if it seems to make the most sense.

The point is that people in the job negotiation process need to become more deliberate and engage in deeper introspection about what they want, what they value, and the kinds of experiences that they are seeking.

• • •

I was coaching someone recently who was changing jobs. His new offer is 10 percent more than he's making now. However, that new job is at the top of the pay scale for his position. When he compares himself to his peers, he should be happy. However, when he goes into this job, he's facing a ceiling.

This brings up a fascinating concept called "the hedonic treadmill." Research has shown that we each have a baseline level of subjective happiness that is independent of specific events. The effects of the hedonic treadmill show up in various areas of our lives: after a time—often three or four years—we adjust to both positive and negative events, and we are no happier or sadder than before those events occurred. This has been shown to be the case in lottery winners, in people who have gotten married, people who have lost a spouse, and even people who have become permanently injured. After three or four years, they are no more or less happy than then were before.

The hedonic treadmill states that the happiness of getting a promotion or a raise is short-lived. After a time, the thrill wears off, and you will have the same level of happiness and satisfaction that you had before the promotion or raise. You've readjusted to the higher income level, and you need another boost in order to feel happy again. Because of the effect of the hedonic treadmill, you will be happier receiving a 10 percent salary increase every year for five years than you would be receiving one big 50 percent increase the first year and no other increases for the next four years. Even though you'd earn more in the second scenario, you'd feel much happier in the first one!

•   •   •

What this tells us is that we can't expect salary increases to automatically make us happier. If we receive a big run-up in pay by landing a new job, that effect is going to wear off after awhile. We know this, too, because of research that shows that money is not a "satisfier" if you're in a job you don't like. However, if you're in a job you do like and you perceive that you aren't being paid adequately, it will be a dissatisfier.

In our work, what ends up making us happy and satisfied is not the money we make, but the struggles and the challenges along the way, how we compare ourselves to others, how successful we feel, and so on. We each have the responsibility of managing our own happiness.

• • •

Of course, there is the other extreme, which is when people are willing take a big salary cut because they want to be doing something else where they know they will be making a bigger contribution and reap more satisfaction from their efforts. So they leave a corporate job making $110,000 a year in order to go into a nonprofit organization to earn $50,000. They're not upset with their compensation because they are doing more interesting things to which they ascribe more meaning and from which they derive greater value.

The ultimate freedom is the executive who says, "Pay me $1 a year because my salary doesn't matter. I have all the money I need. I'm here because I want to make a contribution." Based on the intangibles, he's making more than everyone else.

• • •

So the key concept is more challenge and more impact and more contribution. Then the compensation will follow, but it is not the main consideration.

Research shows that above $30,000 in salary, receiving additional money does not have a significant impact on happiness. Whether someone is making $50,000 or $500,000, the money does not determine happiness. Now, if someone has a job that presents a challenge and enables her to make a contribution and, as an indication of that value, receives $100,000 or $200,000 or $500,000 in compensation, then that's something else. But if all other things are equal, just making more money does not bring more happiness. (Note: Richard Easterlin, economics professor at USC, has written extensively on the subject of the "economics of happiness." In his paper, "Does economic growth improve the human lot," Easterlin concluded that "as a person's income goes up he doesn't grow any happier in a lasting sense." (*http://www.usc.edu/schools/college/news/june_2006/easterlin .html*)

• • •

Let's talk about the person's value to the company.

Going into a job, people may not know precisely how they are going to add value to a company. There is still a lot that they don't know. As they take on the responsibilities of the job, they want to feel as though they are making a difference—that the company is better off because they are working there. That in and of itself is compensation.

People want to know that they have added value, and they should look for ways to determine that they are making a contribution to the company. One way this is accomplished is through performance reviews, which allow people to receive feedback on just exactly how they have made a difference and those areas in which they can develop further to make more of a contribution.

Here's a different way of looking at things, and I'll use my own firm as an example. My clients are attorneys who represent people, many of whom have been injured and now have permanent disabling conditions. These people are our ultimate clients, and their satisfaction with our work is paramount—so much so that we have a guarantee: If you aren't satisfied with our work, you don't owe a fee.

I want to know that the client is satisfied because that gives me satisfaction. There are times when, just as we submit a report to the attorney, we're told the case has been settled. Sure, we'll still earn a fee, but I'd rather have the report really matter than just be compensated for our time.

NEGOTIATING BASED ON YOUR CONTRIBUTION

THE TRAP: You fail to track and communicate the value you add to the organization.

THE LESSON: Too often valuable contributors are not appreciated because they don't communicate to those above them the extent to which they have contributed to the organization's success. If they are quiet and reserved they are likely to be underappreciated and, therefore, undercompensated. Come performance review time, they are also reticent to present a record of the contributions, instead relying solely on their managers' assessment of their work, which could diminish their chances to receive higher compensation and also promotions.

THE TIP: Keep track of your contributions and establish a means of communicating them regularly to your manager and other appropriate people.

As we consider our value to the company, what are some other ways that it is evaluated and recognized?

Public recognition is one, whether it's an award or a mention in the company newsletter. In a fast-food restaurant, you often see the "honor board," where there is a picture and the name of the employee of the week or of the month. That's another form of the value that you receive. It also reflects your value to the company, which we want to be reflected in good salary and good raises, and we also want others to know that we've done well. These are far more valuable to employees than the equivalent amount of permanent salary increases because of the effect of the hedonic treadmill.

•   •   •

This is a whole different track to go down. Most employees want to get paid as much as they can, whether or not the client—in this case, their employer—is satisfied with what they've done or not. Using that analogy, the employee should want the customer—the employer—to be happy and for that happiness to be the basis of how they're paid.

Exactly. It all goes back to the value you bring to the company. The ultimate satisfaction is based on how much positive impact you can have at your job. If I'm an employee and I satisfy my bosses, I will be happier, and I want my success to be reflected in my compensation. But I'm more interested in the employer's satisfaction than in the compensation. That's where my emphasis is. That focus on satisfaction also speaks highly about my value.

•   •   •

My objective in the job negotiation process, then, is to find the job where I can contribute more so that I can get paid more.

The way I like to think about it is that you want to get the most satisfaction from delivering quality in your work, and as a consequence of that you want to get paid well. Money is necessary, but as a "satisfier"—making people happy—it is not sufficient.

•   •   •

This will be a shift in thinking for many people who go into the job offer process looking to maximize their compensation and don't really pay enough attention to the intangibles about the job. Either they don't think about it, or they just assume that

they will have the opportunity to contribute, be mentored, and learn new skills.

There's been a shift in thinking over the past forty or fifty years. Many people are now more interested in job satisfaction than in getting the last dollar of compensation. People are looking at various components of job satisfaction, things like how long their commute will be, whether or not they have flexible time on their job, how much free time it will allow, and other "soft mechanisms" of compensation. In the past, we were just touting salary.

· · ·

So, if one job is fifteen minutes from my home and the other job is an hour from my home, there is a value of that to me, which I have to consider.

People now report that time is a valuable variable. Looking at salaries, adjusted for inflation, people today have three times the earnings capacity of fifty years ago. We have far more ability to buy things than ever before. Therefore, an extra dollar is not worth as much to us as it was fifty years ago. We have gone far beyond our capacity to satisfy our basic means. What we want now are the things that money can't buy—especially time. To do that, we want to avoid a hectic rush hour with flexible time if we can. These are the things that an extra $10,000 or $20,000 in salary can't get you. At a certain level the marginal value of the extra dollar decreases, while the marginal value of other things such as time increases.

In classic economics, the more you have of one thing, the less valuable it becomes. For example, a person might find value in having two or maybe even three cars. But at some point, you won't want another car—even if you could store it for free. The extra car has no value for you.

• • •

What you're saying is, the more money you have the less important it is to get more money.

Yes, relative to the other things that appear to be in shortage, such as free time, money is less important. One of the latest trends in employment data show that more women are taking time off temporarily—one, two, or three years—to raise their children. They are making this decision despite significant economic hardship that it is presenting in terms of the value they would derive (monetarily and otherwise) from being employed. However, they value the time off even more, to the point of being unemployed during the child-raising years.

• • •

Time is a tricky one, though, and a lot of people say, "I want more free time," when that may not actually be what they want. This is where introspection and reflection are absolutely critical, to help people find out what it is they truly want. Unfortunately, most people do not perform this type of analysis well. As soon as they feel discomfort, they want to do something about it, rather than stay with the problem long enough to figure out why they are really dissatisfied.

Using the example of people who says they want more free time, the key question to ask them would be, "To do what?" There may be people who need more time—or perhaps flextime—in order to manage family responsibilities, take care of an elderly parent, attend school, or for some other specific reason. But if all they are going to do with free time is sit in front of a television and zone out, or engage in something else that's completely mind-numbing, then that isn't what they really want.

It may be that they are really unhappy in their job and what they really want is a position with more challenge and difficulty. It might be that what makes them happier isn't free time at all, but a more satisfying and demanding job that requires them to work *longer* hours. They may end up having less free time, but in the end they are happier, more satisfied, and feeling valued because their work is challenging, they are learning and growing, and they know they are making a contribution.

•   •   •

What about security? If we go back fifty years, people stayed with one organization a long time. They were employed by the same company for twenty or more years. Clearly, back then at least, there was some value attached to the idea of security.

People used to stay with one company a long time. At IBM, for example, the tradition was you were employed for life. Today people undergo a number of job transitions. The number of times a person changes jobs has increased significantly over the past fifty years. People no longer have that degree of desire to work for the same company for their entire career. It's more valuable to get diverse experience and to receive different challenges at different corporate cultures. In fact, staying with the same company no longer has anywhere near the same value that it used to have.

•   •   •

If you've been at the same job for a long time, it's not seen as valuable as a diverse set of experience.

41

People wonder why you didn't take the risk and seek out other opportunities.

• • •

Many people at midcareer say that what they really want to do is retire. Their goal—or so they think—is to make enough money so that they don't have to work anymore. What I'm hearing you say throughout this discussion, however, is that this is illusory thinking as it relates to happiness.

A lot of people today are retiring, but then they are going on to a secondary career because the challenge and the satisfaction just isn't there if they aren't working. It isn't just the money; they have enough money. They just don't know what to do with all that time. It seems that we need a smorgasbord: We need the opportunity to work and to have leisure. If we're working all day, every day, we lament that we don't have enough leisure time. If we're retired, we lament not being active.

• • •

Most people haven't thought this through. They think they are working too much, and that they don't want to do this anymore. Most people, however, haven't analyzed the problem well because they haven't asked the right questions about how important it is to be challenged and to make a contribution.

We interview a lot of people about career plans, and most people say that they would have worked or plan to work until they were sixty-five. Few say, I want to work as long as I find the job satisfying or as long as I am physically able and doing well. Age sixty-five might have been a good retirement age thirty-five or fifty years ago when life expectancy wasn't that much past sixty-five. Then it made sense.

When Social Security was first enacted, sixty-five was the average life expectancy, which meant that half the people were dead by that age. Now we're living almost to eighty on the average. The health explosion that we've had is causing us to rethink what we are doing in our fifties and sixties. If the sixties are really the new forties, then we have to look at our career paths and plan not only to work until our early sixties but also into our early or mid-seventies.

•　•　•

What we value in life varies from person to person, depending upon our lives and also the life stage that we're in. Someone who is just starting out may value one thing, while someone at midcareer or later on may value different things.

Think of a person's career path as an arc. Early on a person is ramping up. This is the time usually to strive and achieve and to discover one's own capacity. Young professionals in their twenties, who are just starting out of the box, may focus more on making money and working crazy hours. Farther along that arc, the focus shifts from "How much are you going to give to me" to "How much am I going to give to you." That is a more solid path of happiness and success. The intangibles are valued as much or even more than the tangibles.

•　•　•

Professionals at midcareer who are making six figures are probably looking at their jobs in terms of the value that they are creating. They understand that salary and other forms of compensation are based upon what they are giving to their companies.

Absolutely. People move in their careers from scarcity and needing to make as much money as possible to purpose. It's at the middle and later stages of one's career that there is typically a shift from the pecuniary to the nonpecuniary. Of course, some people will shift earlier than others, and at the other extreme there may be people in their sixties who are still striving like twenty-year-olds making millions of dollars a year as investment bankers.

Understand that there is nothing wrong with money being highly important to a person throughout his or her career. However, the farther along the career arc one goes, the less important money really is. Rather, the money one earns is a consequence of the amount of contribution made and the value one brings to others.

What's the Value to You?

Ask most people about the value of a job, and their first thought is how much it pays. Although compensation is certainly an important consideration when it comes to evaluating a job, there is much more to value. In fact, by removing salary completely from the equation you can see things more clearly. You begin to look at factors such as the satisfaction you derive from being in a job, the opportunities you have to learn new skills and be challenged, the mentoring relationships you established, and so forth.

By looking at the value proposition in a new way, you can assess the job you're in, as well as those you've had in the past. With these insights, you will be more empowered to go after the jobs that meet the criteria of what you see as valuable, while enabling you to showcase the value you bring to the position in order to make a strong case for the six-figure salary you deserve.

TABLE ONE

THE VALUE COMPONENT—YOUR CURRENT JOB

Take your last three positions and rate the value of those positions to you in the following areas. Rate on a scale from 0 to 4, where 0 = Nonexistent or extremely poor, and 4 = Excellent

Value Component	Most Recent Position	Previous Position	Previous Position
Opportunity to be mentored			
Opportunity to mentor others			
Opportunity to contribute			
Opportunity to learn new skills			
Challenge			
Recognition			
Compensation			

Now evaluate any opportunities you are considering:

TABLE TWO

Value Component	#1	#2	#3
Opportunity to be mentored			
Opportunity to mentor others			
Opportunity to contribute			
Opportunity to learn new skills			
Challenge			
Recognition			
Compensation			

CHAPTER THREE

Corporate Culture and You

with Catherine Candland

T he job looks like a perfect opportunity: interesting, challenging, and offering a competitive salary package. Once
on the job, however, you find out that the company
seems to be full of people who are not anything like you. They think,
act, talk, and interact differently. You try to fit in and get along, but
it seems as if you're always on the outside. Your choices are either
to adapt, which becomes more difficult the further you are outside
your comfort zone, or to change jobs—again.

You got into this situation because when you looked at the job
opportunity, you didn't pay enough attention to the "fit factor." If the
corporate culture in a new job isn't the right fit, you'll face the possibility of having to start the process all over again. Sadly, the statistics
bear this out:

During the interview process, Dave Jensen had little insight into
the corporate culture of his future employer. His first two interviews
were by phone, followed by one face-to-face session with a hiring
manager. He did not tour the facility or interact with any employees. The only "intelligence gathering" he conducted was an in-depth
conversation with a consultant/vendor who had worked with the

company. Other than that, Dave was left to discover the corporate culture on his own from the first day on the job.

Luckily for Dave, most of the surprises have been positive. Although the company is bureaucratic and it takes longer than he'd like for decisions to be made, he's pleased with the culture and the way that people interact with each other. "The company has a progressive culture, even though decision-making is slow. They are very change-oriented, and there is good communication within the ranks," he says. "This is also a health-conscious company, and they care about people's development. Had I known all this from the start, I would have been very excited to work here. In fact, if it had turned out that I didn't get this particular job for some reason, I would have kept pursuing opportunities here, knowing that this is a great environment for me."

Corporate culture may be the most important consideration of whether a job is the next right opportunity for you. In fact, determining corporate culture may shape your entire salary negotiation. How much you want to work for a company may affect the compensation you want as well as what you will accept. Further, corporate culture tells you what is most valued in that company. Understanding that will allow you to be more effective in presenting yourself as a good fit and as a valuable contributor in that environment.

In this chapter, Catherine Candland, founder and CEO of Advantage Human Resourcing and a nationally recognized expert in finding the right staff for firms from New York to California, shares techniques for determining what a company's culture is really like, how to determine whether the culture is right for you, and the warning signs of a dysfunctional culture.

With a background in public policy, Cathy has spent her career studying how decisions are made. She brings that experience to the staffing and recruitment industry. In this chapter, she offers expert advice to professionals and managers on finding the right cultural fit.

• • •

How can someone determine the corporate culture of a company?

Corporate culture is revealed in things such as the way work gets done, the values that are manifested in how people communicate and behave, and how decisions get made, both the big and small ones. One big factor determining a person's fit with the corporate culture is work style. The way that work gets done is determined by the culture. Is it an environment that is highly structured with a standard operating procedure for everything that gets done? Is it highly process-oriented with a lot of hierarchy? Or, is the style one in which there is a clear goal and an emphasis on desired outcomes, but a lot of entrepreneurial openness and fewer standard operating procedures? Does the company value disciplined follow-through and playing by the rules, or are people rewarded for bypassing rules to get things done? Although there may be some differences from department to department or division to division, you'll find an overriding value system that drives the majority of behaviors in a company.

• • •

In addition to decision-making and how work gets done, what are some other dimensions of culture that determine how well a person might fit in to an organization?

There are many factors that determine fit and success. For example, is it a warm environment in the workplace, where people smile and interact easily with each other? Or is it a more serious or even tense atmosphere? Do people socialize together after work, or do people rarely, if ever, interact with each other outside of business hours? Do people discuss personal matters with each other, or do they know very little about each other outside of work?

Are there people of different ethnic backgrounds in the company, and do they interact easily with each other? Some organizations are ethnically homogeneous; others have considerable diversity, but members of different ethnic and racial groups cling together. In other organizations, there is significant social interaction between different racial and ethic groups.

How are women treated in the organization? Are the management ranks predominantly male? How easy or difficult is it for women to rise in the company?

•   •   •

Another factor in corporate culture is how conflict is dealt with in the organization.

There are many different styles and behaviors when it comes to conflict. In some organizations, open conflict is avoided, and people seldom give or receive critical feedback—sometimes at significant cost to the organization. In other companies, open conflict and disagreement are encouraged. In some organizations where open disagreement is the norm, there are constructive approaches to resolving conflict. In other organizations, open conflict leads to divisiveness and dysfunction.

•   •   •

Does age play a role in corporate culture?

There are some companies with a very young work force, and if you're in your fifties you might feel as though you are over the hill. In other companies, until you reach a certain age or experience level, you won't be seen as eligible for senior leadership. And some organizations are age-blind. The type of industry often influences the role of age in the corporate culture. Some industries such as advertising and media tend to be more youth oriented, while manufacturing industries tend toward an older work force.

• • •

Are the factors that make up corporate culture easily discernible or are there nuances that you have to discover?

Sometimes it is hard to be concrete because corporate culture is such a complex phenomenon. If you are in the midst of the interview process, one way to discern these things is to ask about how things actually get done in the company. For example, let's say you are interviewing for a business development role. One question would be to ask about the RFP (request for proposal) process. How are decisions made at targeted client companies? What authority does an individual have in pricing practices? Who is on the team? Through this type of questioning, you can discern how work gets done and figure out if you'd be successful in that type of environment.

• • •

Using another example, let's say I'm interviewing for a sales position. I might say to the interviewer: "Walk me through the process when an opportunity arises: A prospect is interested, and I have to come up with a price."

You can apply these types of questions to different types of jobs. Someone interviews for an accounts payable role; that person wants to know what the process looks like for accounts payable. What's working today, and what's not working today. What kind of person succeeds and what kind of person does not succeed in that organization.

NEGOTIATION CULTURE CLASH

THE TRAP: You don't interact with the company according to its cultural norms.

THE LESSON: A large manufacturing company had a team-oriented culture to the point that bonuses were paid on the basis of team performance rather than individual contribution, and everyone on the team received the same bonus. Frances interviewed at the company without first finding out about the culture. Talking to the hiring manager, she focused on her individual contributions to her last employer and never mentioned her contribution to the team. The more she emphasized her individual contribution, the less generous the company was in its negotiation with her because they saw her as a risky fit for their culture.

THE TIP: Understand the culture of the organization and negotiate within its cultural style.

What are some other factors that influence corporate culture, and how can someone find out about them?

Much about corporate culture is related to the explicit and implicit values of the organization. What does the company say in its mission statement? How does this get manifested in the behaviors of the people who work for that organization?

Is there a formal process for decision-making, and if so, around what types of issues and activities? Do managers override decisions? Is entrepreneurial or innovative thinking encouraged and listened to? If so, by whom? All of these questions are good diagnostics that allow an individual to discern what is important to the organization.

• • •

Decision-making within a company reveals a lot about the corporate culture. At one company, it might be a brainstorming session, while at another there is a hierarchical process.

To use an analogy, it's really no different than in a family. One family might be very informal. Everybody lends a hand in the kitchen, and they talk as they put food on the table, continuing the debate and discussion as they eat and clean up afterward. A consensus seems to naturally come about. In another family, different family members state their sides of an argument, and the authority figure makes his or her decision. There is no debate. Companies have similar decision-making dynamics.

Another consideration in corporate culture is whether there is consistency in the way that decisions are made at the senior and middle management levels. In one company, you may have an internal team that is united and aligned, and decisions are made the same way throughout the organization.

In another, there may be some inconsistencies in style and alignment, resulting in a quite different culture. Other cultures are characterized by political infighting, where it is important for people to protect their turf. If you're not good at fighting and if you can't protect your turf, then you will not do well here. You wouldn't want to put someone in that environment who works best in a more cooperative culture.

• • •

To make this type of assessment, a prospective employee needs to get out of the realm of whether an environment is "good" or "bad" and look at how the environment functions.

There are absolutely great people with great values in all types of environments. The issue is fit.

•   •   •

The issue of fit should be addressed before someone begins to explore job opportunities. This is not something that people should begin to consider when they're in the middle of negotiations. One way to become educated is to analyze the culture of their current employers.

Yes, and the same issues apply. The recurring theme is how decisions are made, and on what values and criteria are those decisions based. I would look at the work style of the organization. Is it highly structured, very process driven, standardized and scaleable, or is it ad hoc and highly entrepreneurial, with a decentralized decision-making process? Put together a list of adjectives and adverbs that describe the culture and how work gets done. Then contrast that with other cultures and environments that you'd like to investigate.

The hours that people work is another issue. What are the expectations? Are you expected to be on the job all the time, or is working remotely allowed? In some companies, there is a value system that if you are not in the office, you are not working. In other environments, people don't have to be in the office to get work done; a premium is placed on output versus being onsite. In the interview process, there are many questions to ask about how work is done, which provide clues about the corporate culture.

•   •   •

What can you determine from observing other people at the company?

Seek out opportunities to talk with people in the company. The way they describe the environment will also help you see the culture. Find out what kind of person succeeds in that company and what kind of person doesn't succeed.

Another approach is to ask about the person who had the job for which you're interviewing. Why did that person leave? What was that person's profile, experience, and skill set? How long was the last person in the job? Has there been repetitive turnover in this position? In a highly structured environment, jobs don't change that much. In a more innovative one, there may be newly created jobs. You can get a sense of the style of the organization from these types of questions.

These questions may also help you determine the likely speed of promotions. Do people move across job functions in this organization, or are they restricted to function in one area? Are managers promoted from within the company or are they brought in from the outside?

●   ●   ●

For some people, however, the interview process is limited to conversations with human resources and/or the hiring manager. Can someone get an accurate read on corporate culture with such limited interactions?

As you go through the interview process, you may only see two or three people. You may not have a chance to shadow anyone or spend any time with the team that you would be working with, or even speak with a number of different people in the organization. In these situations it will be difficult to calibrate the environment to see if you can picture yourself there.

To get a fuller picture, you can't rely on just your interactions with one or two people. In a good interview process, you will have three to five experiences with the company. You can tell a lot by observing. Go into the company cafeteria, and see if people are sitting together in small groups, talking and interacting, or if they tend to sit by themselves. What do you observe in the hallways and elevators?

· · ·

I was at a hospital recently installing a performance management system, and as I walked down the hall to the HR department, everyone I passed who worked for the hospital said hello to me. It gave me the feeling that this was a friendly place. Then I found out that, on their performance reviews, one of the things they are evaluated on is saying hello to people.

There are many ways to calibrate the culture. You can get a sense very quickly whether people are enjoying being there and imagine how you would feel in that environment. This doesn't mean that you have to conduct three to five formal assessment processes to determine the culture. You can learn a tremendous amount by asking a few open-ended questions and obtaining a good feel for what the culture and environment are like.

· · ·

It's also helpful to have conversations with people completely outside the interview process. When a company wanted to recruit me for a senior management position, the first thing I did was go into my network to find somebody who worked there. We had a conversation about what it was like to work at that company. The purpose was not for him to evaluate me but to give me some deep background about the culture and the work environment.

People who work there or who used to work there are great sources of information, as are clients who work with the company. You want to cast a broad net of intelligence. Through technology and the Internet, we do have the ability to get more information about companies. But I still think there is huge value in the relationship network.

THE DANGER OF A BAD CULTURE FIT

THE TRAP: You're unhappy and unappreciated in a corporate culture in which you don't fit.

THE LESSON: John was a highly seasoned executive brought into the company from a different industry to increase sales. The organization, however, had an "insider culture." Everyone in the company had been in the industry for a long time, and there was a cultural belief that if someone didn't have long-term industry knowledge, that person couldn't contribute. John was ostracized and not given a chance to succeed.

THE TIP: Know what you're getting into.

What happens if someone ends up with a new job that is a bad fit culturally?

When you're not aligned with the culture, the stress in the job goes up extraordinarily. In my opinion, the sooner that you're out of those situations the better. There is a whole recovery process that you'll have to go through to regain your sense of who you are. It's no different than being in a dysfunctional relationship; it may take awhile afterward to get back to a place where you feel good about who you are and what you want.

• • •

As part of the job search process, someone may be looking outside of what has been her usual job or industry. What are the considerations regarding fit?

First, you need to think about what are your real skills and experiences, in order to accurately evaluate yourself and what you've done. Then, look at the type of opportunities that would allow you to leverage those skills and experiences. For example: you have the skills to be a paralegal, but you don't like being a paralegal; if that's the only job you look at you will be back in the same trap. Instead, as you look at your job, ask yourself, what skills and experience do I have as a paralegal that I could leverage or parlay into other areas? Some of the best placements that our firm has made have been outside a person's typical job type or industry sector into something completely different. The questions to ask yourself are: What are my skills and experiences, and where could they possibly be applied in the marketplace that I haven't thought about before?

• • •

As part of your skills and experience assessment, you also need to ask yourself what environment would be the best fit for you, where you would really flourish.

Where do you feel comfortable, and where do you feel that you belong? In addition to liking what you do every day, do you like how it feels in the environment? Do you feel it's appropriately aligned with where you are comfortable?

There are also situations where the process of decision-making or how the work gets done is very different from what people are used to, but they feel as if they really do belong. They have such an affinity for the group and the company that they are able to adapt.

Where people struggle—even if they have all the skills and experience and are motivated—is in situations in which they feel they can't fit into the environment. They feel as if they are an outlier, and they are unhappy there.

•   •   •

When there isn't alignment, you can feel upset day in and day out. You say to yourself, "I have to go to work, and it's horrible," because you're not in the right place.

There is a gut feeling that you have to pay attention to. It's like when high school kids tour colleges, and they can be on a campus for ten minutes and say, "I don't see myself here." As we get older, however, we often overanalyze and don't trust our intuitive sense of what is right for us.

Our company has a three-step formal process for determining if a candidate is right for our work environment. First, we assess and validate the person's experience and skills. We test their competence to determine if they have the skills and experience to do the job. Second, we want to find out what motivates them and what excites them. Are the tasks and responsibilities aligned with their motivation?

Third—and this is the most important part of the interview, which is conducted by a senior-level person—is the notion of "fit." It is an assessment based on a detailed walk-through of the day-to-day job with the candidate. We try to make the job and the corporate culture very transparent to the candidate. For example, in our offices we don't have many individual offices. People work in an open environment. If you prefer an environment with privacy, you would not work well in this setting. If you feed off the energy of others and you pick up intelligence through osmosis in that bullpen environment and through the camaraderie of having people around you, you would be a better fit. We want our candidates to experience our environment, and we both evaluate whether they will do well in it.

If you can, spend twenty minutes shadowing people who are doing the same or a similar job to see if you will fit in the environment. It's in the best interest of the company to make the reality of the job transparent to the candidate to the degree that it is humanly possible.

• • •

What happens for a lot of people in middle-manager positions is that they've been recruited. They have not been actively looking at other jobs. They get excited about the opportunity that they're being recruited for and they don't ask these questions.

In the majority of situations, people do not have one or two other competing alternatives. The problem is people often don't make the right decisions if they only have one option. It's a challenge. If you are in one job and you are looking for another one, it's hard to come up with two other opportunities.

One thing you can do is to analyze the corporate culture of your current or past work environments and see how well you fit in those environments. You can then compare those environments to the corporate culture in the job and organization you are considering.

• • •

There is one particular situation that I would like you to address: People working for large companies who are interested in or are recruited for start-ups and entrepreneurial companies. Smaller and middle-market companies are always talking to

people who work for large corporations. One of the key ques-tions is whether this person will thrive in a smaller company environment.

When someone moves from a large company to a middle-market or smaller firm, one issue is that they have been used to having a strong infrastructure around them. Often there are many rules in a large firm about how work gets done and how decisions are made. In smaller firms, they will likely find less structure and fewer resources, which can be a real challenge. In some cases, it's a skill set issue; they don't have the decision-making experience to work effectively in an environment in which there is not the same hierarchy and process. However, it can also go the other way. Some people are tired of the structure of a large firm and find that it was really inhibiting their entrepreneurial spirit. They find a smaller company refreshing.

Again, the questions that people should ask themselves in these situations are: How are decisions made in the entrepreneurial envi-ronment? How is work done? What resources will I have? What are the differences between large company environments and the one I am considering? To the degree that people can get specific about corporate culture and what they want, they can make informed deci-sions about what is right for them.

• • •

What about when someone has been working for one com-pany for a long time? Are there special considerations in this situation?

For people who have been in jobs longer than eight years, the sta-tistics bear out that their first move typically lasts less than twenty-four months and is usually not the right move. The move after that is more likely the optimal one.

If you've been with one company for a long time, it is important to understand its corporate culture and how you fit in that culture. What works for you in the culture? What doesn't work for you? If you analyze your corporate culture and your fit with it, you will be more likely to ask the right questions about an opportunity with another company. You want to ensure as much as possible that you're not walking into an environment that doesn't work for you.

•   •   •

Often, candidates aren't aware of how decisions are made and how the organization operates. They don't think about the underlying values in the culture and how they affect decisions and how the organization operates. However, this is a very important self-reflective step. For example, if a company says, "We get products to our customers as fast as we can, and quality is secondary," that's not good or bad. You just have to understand that's a key value in the organization. If you know that you hate doing something that is not of the highest quality, it will be a difficult place for you to work.

Also, there are the stated culture and values, and then there are the operating values. They may or may not have much to do with each other. As a prospective employee, your job is to understand the difference. What do people say that they do, and what do they really do? Using your example of the hospital that you visited, there may be a practice of saying hello to visitors in the hallway. If it's not aligned with the practices in the cafeteria and the operating room, then you have a surface execution that is not engrained into the fiber of the organization. It's not a bad thing, but you need to know.

•   •   •

Another perspective that I find fascinating is the influence of the personality, style, and values of the top leaders on corporate culture. This is certainly true for entrepreneurial organizations and middle-market companies. The policies and beliefs of the CEO filter down through the whole organization. If the CEO has been there awhile, people want their decisions and actions to please him, and that trickles down through the ranks of the company. If a new CEO is brought in who has a different perspective or different values than the previous CEO, you can often watch the organization and see an almost immediate shift in attitude and culture. Sometimes people will want to remain there and sometimes not.

The case of a founder who is CEO and has taken the company to a certain threshold is different from the CEO of a large company brought in by the board. The role of the CEO of an ongoing large institution is influenced by the fact that there is a well-defined culture already in place. Sometimes the culture of a large company will "expel" a new CEO the way antibodies attack a foreign substance in the body. Culture has a powerful effect.

•   •   •

Another area where culture plays a key role is mergers and acquisitions. We know that one of the primary reasons mergers and acquisitions fail is that corporate culture was not taken into account. People leave or become unmotivated in the acquired company because the culture of the acquiring firm is so different. These are considerations for prospective employees if the company they are looking at is going through a merger or acquisition or has had a change in top management.

In the case where a smaller company is acquired by a much larger one, the culture of the larger company usually prevails. People in the acquired company frequently do not want to change their culture to fit with the larger, more bureaucratic one, and you have a recipe for disaster. This is one of the main reasons why so many acquisitions fail.

A similar problem occurs in mergers where the two merger companies have different cultures. The clash between the cultures can outweigh the benefits gained through increased efficiencies and synergies from the merger. If you are considering joining a company that has recently merged or been acquired, these concerns should be of paramount importance to you.

$$\bullet \quad \bullet \quad \bullet$$

So, if you are a candidate for a job with a small company that has been acquired by a larger firm, you may find yourself in the middle of a major change and cultural transition.

Or, it may be the best opportunity and the most incredible learning experience that you could imagine. You have to assess if that is the competency you are looking to build. Do you like to live in that kind of turmoil and provide functional value to a firm during transition?

I know of a firm that went through the interviewing process with a candidate who would be a fabulous fit for the environment and has all the right skills. The employer, however, was in the midst of being acquired by another company. Management felt they owed it to him to let him know about the reality of the situation and what it could look like. They played out best, worst, and middle-case scenarios. It became very clear that he would actually thrive in that type of opportunity. What it would take to make it work for the team was valuable for the next phase of his career. This kind of openness also breeds an incredible amount of trust, which for some people is a critical fit factor.

In some cultures, there are a lot of secrets. People aren't told what's going on until the eleventh or twelfth hour. For some people that may be fine; they don't want to be involved. Others feel vulnerable and excluded. For a middle manager, this is an important consideration about the culture that you're walking into with a new job.

•   •   •

In some environments there may be cross-cultural issues in terms of an operation in one country and management or ownership in another. These differences affect communications style and approach. How does this impact a job opportunity where someone may be interacting, internally or externally, with people from different national or geographic cultures?

A person may be moving to a different part of the world or dealing with a different customer base. The greater the difference in cultures, the more important the assessment of the corporate culture. It still comes down to the way decisions get made and why they get made. You must understand the depth and breadth of all the fit factors.

•   •   •

What about increased diversity in the workplace? American senior management has historically been white and male. At the middle-management level especially we're seeing more women and people of color.

Today's workplace has diversity factors and also generational factors. People who are more mature sometimes are challenged working with kids out of college who do all their communicating via text messages, who think quickly on their feet, and who are technologically savvy. The younger employees were brought up with the mindset of

"What are we going to do this minute?" versus the generation that is more thoughtful and likes to gather information more sequentially. Cultural adaptations to diversity and gender issues get rolled up into how decisions are made and respected. People end up blending and jelling in a way that's fascinating to watch.

•   •   •

What is your advice for companies and managers that want to create a diverse work environment?

One thing that many people have to work on is the tendency to want to hire people who are like them. They have to make sure, if diversity is a goal of the company, that the recruitment process supports it. A diverse workplace is a more interesting and fun place to work.

For example, our payroll department is made up of one of the most diverse groups of people you can imagine. That team works so well together. One of the ways that they deal with their diversity is through the music they listen to. They consciously try to make it appeal to one group, then another, and then another. One day you'll go in that department and they're playing classical; another day it will be rap. It also reflects the way they collaborate. In fact, it works so well that this group gets together and socializes on weekends—and this is not a group that you could imagine getting together outside of work.

•   •   •

If you look at career as a major part of our life journey, then what you are talking about is self-knowledge. You need to look at what really matters to you. At the beginning of one's career, a person may be naive. There is the allure of the big investment-banking firm, for example, which has such a high status. Some-

one who is bright and aggressive and competitive may think this is it. Then they find out that it's not for them. And so we go forward.

The readers of this book, who are in the midst of six-figure salary negotiation, probably are at a point where they should be looking at who they really are, and what really matters to them. With this knowledge, they have to decide where they are going to thrive and feel satisfied, and what type of environment will help them flourish. The degree to which they can be thoughtful while moving through the recruitment and negotiation process is really important. This is why I was so fascinated with this business in the first place. I wanted to learn why people chose certain things and what facilitated their choice process. I am interested in what is productive and meaningful for people and what determines their experience, so that the outcome is a positive one.

This discussion really underscores how important it is to understand the culture of a company before you even think about negotiating compensation.

Understanding Corporate Culture

The job looks interesting, the salary is attractive, and the opportunity appears to advance your career path. Should you go for it? At the six-figure salary level, there is more than money at stake. With a position that probably carries a lot of responsibilities and expectations, commensurate with the salary level, you need to know if this is an environment in which you will thrive. That's not to say a company is "good" or "bad," but rather whether it's the right culture for you. Remember, the higher up in a company you go and the bigger salary you're commanding, the more that's riding on each position you take. Therefore, assessing corporate culture will help you to determine the positions that will be the best fit, while allowing you to demonstrate to the hiring manager that you, too, are aligned with the company environment. The better the fit for both parties, the stronger your negotiating position.

To learn about and understand a corporate culture, answer the following questions. To begin, answer the questions for your current or most recent employer.

- What adjectives would you use to describe the culture?
- What adjectives would you use to describe people who succeed at the organization?
- What adjectives would you use to describe people who do not succeed at the organization?
- How are decisions made in the organization? Are they made by consensus? By a senior authority figure? By committee?
- What hours do employees tend to work at the company?
- Do people often work from home?
- Is it a warm or cold environment?
- Is open conflict and disagreement encouraged or avoided?
- Is there a lot of political infighting in the company?
- Are there people from different ethnic backgrounds at the company, and how do they interact?
- How are women treated in the organization?
- What is the company dress code? Is it formal? Casual?
- Do people socialize together after work and share news and details about their personal lives?
- Are there standard operating procedures for everything, or do people regularly bypass rules?
- Is innovation highly valued in the organization?
- Do people work in private offices or in open spaces? Is the environment quiet or noisy?
- What is the personality and work style of the CEO? Of the management team?

- How has the culture changed over the past ten or fifteen years? How is it changing now?

Now go back and answer the same questions based on your own personality, work style preferences, and values.

CHAPTER FOUR

What's Your Market?

with Donald Delves

A s you look for the next right job, you enter the job market. Just as that term implies, there are forces of supply and demand that come into play when you negotiate your job offer. No matter how unique your skills, experience, and knowledge may be, the job negotiation process is influenced by market conditions. Therefore, you need to know the market for your position, taking into consideration your skill set, experience level, and even your geographic region. Without a realistic understanding of your market, you will not negotiate to the best possible outcome.

There's a joke in recruiting circles that illustrates this concept:

A recent college graduate approaches a recruiter. "What I'm looking for," the graduate says, "is a job with a $100,000-a-year salary to start."

The recruiter responds: "Would you also like six weeks' vacation?"

"That would be great," the candidate replies.

"How about a corner office?" the recruiter goes on.

"Absolutely," the candidate says.

"I suppose you'd like a Ferrari as a company car?"

"You've got to be joking!" the candidate gasps.

"Yes," the recruiter replies, "but you started it."

Not knowing your job market is no laughing matter. Even as a serious candidate, you can blow yourself out of the water by asking for too much, and you can damage your career by asking for too little. I've seen people lose out on getting a position for which they were qualified because they didn't value themselves accurately.

Dave Jensen's only salary gauge was his previous job, which—as explained in Chapter 1—was actually above the market. Focusing on the salary figure alone, Dave says he didn't ask any questions about the grade level of his job or where he was being paid within that grade (meaning above or below the midpoint). "All I was told was that the position paid 'X,' and they weren't able to pay more than that," Dave recalls.

Dave also did not understand some of the key dynamics of compensation. He did not try to convince the hiring manager of his value so that the manager would agree to pay him more—and then go to the HR department to make it happen.

These insights and others are explained in this chapter by Donald Delves, founder of The Delves Group, one of the premier executive compensation consulting firms in the country. Don discusses the importance of knowing your market—and how to find out what your market is.

As an executive compensation consultant, Don advises boards of directors of *Fortune* 1000 firms, as well as management and senior executive teams, on how to pay people, how to structure compensation and incentive packages, and how to measure and reward performance in order to ensure that the company is getting a return for its investment in senior management. He is also the author of *Stock Options and the New Rules of Corporate Accountability: Measuring, Managing and Rewarding Executive Performance* (Second Edition), and *CCH Accounting for Compensation Arrangements* (2006).

• • •

In job negotiations, the danger of asking for too much money appears obvious: you want more than the company is willing to pay. But what about when you don't ask for enough compensation? What message does that send?

I'll give you an example from very early in my career. It was 1980, and I was coming out of the University of Chicago, Graduate School of Business. The university published a list of all the offers and acceptances reported by graduates. At the time, the University of Chicago and Harvard were definitely at the top of the market, which was probably $28,000 or $30,000 for a job in banking. Overall, most of the offers and acceptances in banking were around $22,000 to $25,000, and if someone went to New York City the salary might have been a bit more.

My first employer out of graduate school initially offered me $23,000. I asked for $25,000, and I ended up getting $24,000, which was good money in 1980. The company's reaction to my counter-offer throughout this negotiation process was very positive. It reflected the fact that they could see I was an aggressive, assertive guy. After they hired me, they told me that they liked that I countered with a higher offer.

• • •

Your employer thought that you would use those negotiation skills on the company's behalf. You demonstrated your ability to ask for better terms.

As an employee, I showed I could push on the bank's behalf—maybe an extra ten basis points on a loan. The important thing in this type of negotiation, however, is that what you're asking for has to be within an acceptable range. You have to know what market you are stepping into. That means determining the competitive market for your talent and the job that you're going after.

•   •   •

Let's say that I want to pursue a job that I've heard about, or, that company has contacted me. At this point, as I'm contemplating making my next move, how do I know what my market is?

That's a very good question. In my business as a compensation consultant, I look at data all the time to figure out the salary structure and pay levels at a company. In my field there are consultants in compensation, benefits, actuarial services, health and welfare, and each of these firms conducts in-depth and detailed surveys of how companies pay for hundreds of different jobs. Hundreds if not thousands of companies submit data to consulting firms, who assimilate this data into surveys. The survey results are then sold to companies so that they can ascertain the trends in compensation. As a job candidate, you're not going to see the in-depth data that I have access to, but you should know that it exists.

•   •   •

Take a moment and tell us about these consulting surveys.

The surveys are quite sophisticated. Let's say that 300 companies have submitted data on compensation for one type of position, for example a Level Three engineer. Based on that data, the median pay will be calculated, as well as the twenty-fifth percentile and the seventy-fifth percentile. Sometimes the surveys will show more details, such salary plus bonus (which is total cash compensation), as well as long-term incentives such as stock options and restricted stock (which will be addressed later in this chapter). Then, the survey will show total direct compensation consisting of salary, bonus, and long-term incentives.

In addition, the surveys will sort that data into various "buckets," such as by industry. You'll be able to look at all Level Three engineers, then see what a person in that position would be paid in telecommunications or the automotive industry or by region if that's a significant factor. Higher-level positions are usually considered to be a national market, with the same compensation no matter if a person works in Arkansas or New York City. However, there can be regional differences and anomalies. For example, an engineer in San Jose, where there is a relatively high cost of living and a remarkable assemblage of engineering companies, probably makes more than an engineer in, say, Tallahassee.

•   •   •

It's good to know that this data exists, and the company recruiting me or thinking of hiring me has access to that data and is using it to determine the salary I'm going to be offered. There is a wealth of data upon which my offer is based, not just some internal pay structure within the company. Since most people won't have access to the kind of in-depth compensation surveys that companies pay for, how can they become educated about the salary ranges for their job?

Information is available online at sites such as *salary.com*. There are also less formal surveys that are available from professional or trade magazines and associations. You can do a Web search for your job title and salary and gather information from a variety of sources.

When you are negotiating with the company, you can now take this data and explain that you've been doing some research. You might say, for example, "I'm a member of a professional society of engineers that produces a study on salaries in the field. That study says an engineer at my level should be making $85,000 to $95,000 in salary, plus bonus, and that the vast majority of people at my level are getting stock options." This discussion may actually open up the company's data to you. The company may tell you about the surveys and data sources that it uses and what the findings of that data are. However, they are not going to tell you about that market data unless you ask.

• • •

What would the company's reaction be to someone bringing in information about salary surveys? Not only are you trying to negotiate a better offer for yourself, but you're using industry data and surveys to back it up.

Admittedly, it could be a double-edged sword. You do run the risk of being perceived as a "pain." The whiner's lament is always "I'm underpaid." However, I would still do it. At the very least, you have to find the data and do your homework in order to find out what the market is for your position. It also comes down to how you use this information. You need to show that you know what you're talking about. The way you present yourself also does matter.

Another way to find out about the market is to shop around. Too many people interview with one or two companies and take one job. If you're going to change positions, you should interview with seven, eight, or nine companies and find out what they are paying. That's the market, and more specifically, that's the market for you based on which companies are interested in you and what they are willing to pay you.

Traps,
Lessons,
& Tips

ASKING FOR MORE MONEY

THE TRAP: You assume the maximum salary number quoted to you by HR is fixed in stone and cannot be changed.

THE LESSON: You're told the pay range is a bottom of X and to a top of Y, and you're making more than the top figure in your current job. When you explain this to HR, the representative tells you: "Sorry, we can't pay you more than Y."

THE TIP: Contact the hiring manager and tell her that HR told you the maximum salary for the job is Y, and you are currently making more than that. Point out that you know in some companies exceptions are occasionally made in circumstances like this, and ask if that is possible at this company. By doing so, you are empowering the hiring manager to advocate on your behalf.

It's analogous to putting your house on the market. You're looking at lots of comparable houses (comps). You don't just look at one or two houses. What else should someone consider to determine their market for a particular job and salary level?

The first place to start is to know where you are coming from. What is the salary structure that you are leaving? What is the range of salary for the job you currently have, and where do you fall in that range? There is no reason to wait until you start the job hunt to find out this information; you should know beforehand where you sit in your current job structure.

• • •

How do you find out that information?

Ask. You can start with human resources, and in most companies you will readily be told this information. There are some companies whose philosophy is not to tell employees that information, but those situations are rare today. You should be told the salary range and midpoint. With that information, you can determine where you are in relation to the overall range and the midpoint.

In fact, ideally you should know the whole salary structure of your organization, or at least from where you are on up. That includes the job grades and salary ranges from your level to the next level and all the way up to where you aspire to be. In a consulting firm, for example, you may be an associate consultant. The next level is senior consultant, and after that manager, then principal, and then partner. If that's your goal, you should know what the job grades and salary range are for each of those levels.

• • •

Let's take a step back and talk about why companies have these kinds of structures. Can you elaborate?

Back in the 1940s, 1950s, and 1960s, as companies became increasingly large, complex, and bureaucratic, with more people doing many different kinds of jobs, they needed more structure and organization. Companies couldn't just hire people and pay whatever they thought they should pay them. If they did, it would be very easy to lose track, with massive pay discrepancies and many jealous employees. Plus, a company could end up paying people too much.

The solution was the traditional company organization, which is a pyramid of many layers. Each layer reports to the next layer, and every layer has its own salary level or range. Sometimes a layer may have two or three salary levels in it. Engineering, accounting, human resources, and many nonoperating functions in an organization typically have clearly defined levels. You start as an engineer 1, 2, or 3, and then you become a supervising engineer 1, 2, and 3, and after that a managing engineer 1, 2, and 3. Each level is assigned a job grade, and each grade has a midpoint, minimum, and maximum salary.

•   •   •

How wide, or narrow, would a typical salary range be?

Typically, in a salary range, the minimum would be 80 percent of the midpoint, and the maximum would be 120 percent of the midpoint. In addition, each job grade has a midpoint that is 15 percent above the next lower midpoint. This is the typical, standard structure.

•   •   •

Knowing where you are in a salary range reveals a lot about your career path. It also shows what obstacles or challenges you could face on that path. For example, a person I know was recently hired by a bank. He was told that he is at the highest grade for a nonmanager, and he's at the top of that salary range. When he explained this to me, he wondered if this was good for him or not.

That situation would make me very nervous. It sounds like the classic recipe for someone never making any more money unless he is able to penetrate the barrier of getting promoted to the next level. If that were being offered to me, my reaction would be, "You are bringing me in at the top of the highest level you can pay me without making me a manager. That tells me I am never going to make more money than what is given to me now, except for cost-of-living adjustments, until I am promoted to become a manager. You're also telling me that I'm not manager material yet, otherwise you'd hire me as a manager."

●　　●　　●

Is it possible that he is making more than some of the managers there?

Yes, it's very possible that he is actually being paid more than what some of the lower-level managers are being paid. These kinds of structures usually overlap by design. If he's already making more money than the lowest-level managers—but they are managers and he's not—then the message to him is he has skill sets that make him valuable, but he's still a highly paid technician. He's in the far upper right-hand corner of a box that has some firm lines around it. In order to receive any significant increase in compensation, he's going to have to become a manager.

●　　●　　●

We have been talking about promotion as a means to increase pay. What are the other ways employees increase their pay without changing employers?

There are three ways that a company will typically increase someone's pay: cost-of-living adjustments, merit raises, and promotions. Let's look at the first one. Cost-of-living or inflation adjustments usually move up the whole salary structure every year by some increment tied to inflation. It's usually low, like 1 percent. Secondly, companies have a merit increase budget. In addition to whatever cost-of-living increases have been budgeted, there is a merit increase budget for people who have contributed to or improved performance. Based on individual performance, one person may get a 5 percent merit increase, another person a 7 percent increase, and someone else gets a 2 percent increase.

•   •   •

Can you give an example of how a merit raises are given out?

The best way is to show you a grid.

TABLE THREE

MERIT RAISE/PERFORMANCE TABLE

		Ranking in Salary Range			
		Top Quartile	2nd Quartile	3rd Quartile	Bottom Quartile
Performance Ranking	Top Quartile	2%	3%	5%	7%
	2nd Quartile	1%	2%	3%	5%
	3rd Quartile	0%	1%	2%	3%
	Bottom Quartile	0%	0%	0%	0%

The higher your ranking, the greater your merit increase, and the lower your ranking, the lower your merit increase. If you're a high performer with a low ranking in your salary range, you're likely to receive one of the larger percentage merit increases; for example, 7 percent. On the other hand, a high performer who has topped out in salary range may only be able to get a 2 percent raise. The reason is that a company generally does not want to pay people above their range. They may allow it, in which case you'll be known as a "red circle"—indicating that you're being paid above the range, but it's an exception that most companies don't like. The third way that you can get a pay increase is to be promoted in order to jump out of your old range and into a new one.

•   •   •

As a potential or incoming employee, it would be good to know what kind of "grid" I fit into in terms of my pay range.

Ideally, you'd want to know what the salary structure is and where you are in that salary structure. I recall in my early days working for a large compensation consulting firm, I was given a very nice promotion that bumped me up into the consultant range. It turned out to be very good for me because there was a lot of room for my salary to move up within my pay range. In the first few years after that promotion I was given big raises based on my performance. I didn't understand the mechanics of the merit raise grid at the time.

•   •   •

You knew that you were getting these raises on merit, but you didn't know that the company was able to reward you so well because you had lots of room to move. You were at the lower end of the salary range at the time.

Exactly, because once someone gets to the top of the salary range, the company has to justify why you are being paid more than others. And that sets up the scenario of other people complaining, "I heard that So-and-So is getting paid $92,000 and I'm making $87,000. Why is that person so great?" Companies don't want to have that conversation—especially if the reason is that one person is performing better than another. They'd rather give the person a promotion, in which case the salary doesn't need to be justified.

• • •

What about in smaller companies that are not so bureaucratic? It's possible in these organizations that pay does not correlate to anything other than level of capability or performance.

If a company doesn't have job grades or salary ranges, then the first thing I would ask is why. It may be the company's philosophy. They may want to be more freeform and have general levels in the organization, while still being a "flat organization"—meaning they don't see the need for a lot of levels. In a traditional bureaucracy, there are many hierarchical levels. In a flat organization there are fewer levels, and managers typically will have more direct reports. In a hierarchical bureaucracy with many levels it's easier to track your career progression. In a flat organization it is more difficult to identify career paths. There may be one typical career path, or there may be dual tracks, one technical and one managerial.

There are also modern and highly creative fluid organizations like Apple Computer, with few levels. Your whole career could be one adventure of going from one project to another. People in those organizations typically have a different set of goals; instead of being promoted, they go from one cool project to the next one.

• • •

Let's go back to the example of my friend who was hired at the top of the salary range for nonmanagers at the bank. In his case, HR volunteered this information. How should he have responded?

The next question would be, "What do I have to do to get into the next salary range?" If the answer is, become a manager, then he needs to ask about the criteria for becoming a manager. Also, he would want to know what it is about him and his experience level that the company doesn't currently see him as a manager.

• • •

It may be that the company has a specific number of manager slots, and there aren't any open slots. And if that's the case, he would want to know how many people are queued up for the manager's slot.

He would also want to find out his chances of being promoted into a manager's slot within the next six months to a year. That means finding out how many openings are anticipated, how many people are in line for those openings, and how it is decided who gets promoted. He could even ask, "What's my competition?"

• • •

When this person was offered this job, he had two choices. He could go to the bank with a job being paid at the top of the grade as a nonmanager and have some uncertainty as to when he might be considered for a promotion to manager. Or he could stay where he was, which he felt was a dead-end job. He had been passed over for a promotion a few times. One of his peers was now his manager. He could see that it would be very hard for him to move up in his current firm. What did that tell him about the market choices he was now facing?

Generally speaking, the rule of thumb is you don't change jobs unless you are getting a promotion. In this situation, the person was dead-ended and was willing to take a lateral move in order to have a better chance of moving up in the future.

• • •

If there is a rule of thumb about getting a promotion with a job change, is there another rule of thumb regarding salary increases and job change?

If you're getting a sizeable promotion, you might get as much as 30 percent increase. For middle-market jobs, you might expect a 15 to 20 percent increase in salary. A 15 percent increase is typically a one-grade promotion, while a 30 percent increase is a two-grade promotion. If you get a 20 percent increase, then you have probably made a one-grade move, but you are moving higher up in that grade.

• • •

How does the pace of promotion vary from industry to industry, or market to market?

Here's an example from my own career. The upward path at the bank where I worked out of graduate school was slow and not well defined. It was governed in a larger way than I was comfortable with by how well a person was perceived. After I left the bank, I went to an accounting firm, which was an "up or out" type of organization. Every one to two years you were either promoted or you were asked to leave. Personally, I liked that game better than "We'll keep you here forever, but you might not get promoted, depending upon whether or not we like you." At the time, I wasn't sure where I wanted to go, but I didn't want to stagnate. At the accounting firm, I knew that in four or five years I would at least be a manager or I would be out.

•   •   •

**By the time people are involved in the six-figure salary negotia-
tion, they are further along in their career. How can they judge
the opportunities and pace of promotion and salary advances
at this level, given their market place?**

When I was at this level, I was at a compensation consulting firm. As
a technician, I was considered to be the best person in that office, and
one of the best at the firm in terms of what I did. I was at the highest
level of what they could pay me in my job grade. The promotions
that had come quickly at first had slowed down. A colleague of mine
was promoted, and I wasn't. I asked a lot of questions as to why this
happened, and finally I was given an explanation. There were several
key competencies in that organization, and I was at the top of the
competency range for technical proficiency. I was at the middle for
being able to manage and delegate. But I was at the bottom for being
able to generate new business. In order to be promoted, I needed to
be at the middle or higher in the competency range for generating
new business. This was a real "eureka" moment for me.

•   •   •

**This is an important point. You didn't just get resentful or tell
yourself, "I'm out of here" when your colleague was promoted
and you weren't. You intended to understand why. You learned
the criteria for being promoted in your particular market and
then set in motion a development plan for yourself in order to
be promoted. This included asking difficult questions and finding out things that were unpleasant for you to hear. Yet, that
was a turning point in your career. The lesson is you found out**

why you weren't promoted. You pursued that question until you received an answer that felt real and truthful to you.

I had a choice: I could remain as a top-quality technician, in which case there were fewer opportunities for promotion that would come more slowly, or I could learn how to sell and generate new business. I chose the latter. It took me a year to become a decent salesperson and generate new business. The first year I generated $400,000 in new business. This was a time when a partner was doing $1.5 million in new business. The second year, I generated $800,000 in new business, and I was considered effective.

•   •   •

How did you develop the skills that you needed?

I invested in executive coaching and sales training. I devoted energy and resources to reach my goal. In addition to an external coach to teach me how to sell, I also had internal mentors at the firm who showed me how to sell. I also found a couple people at my level who were in similar circumstances, and we buddied up to generate business together. At the firm, there was a belief that technical people were not strong salespeople. Someone who was a dyed-in-the-wool technician generally was not seen as being capable of becoming a good salesperson. I wasn't breaking organization rules by becoming an effective salesperson, but I was breaking organizational beliefs—even though I was doing exactly what they wanted me to do.

•   •   •

After the second year, when you generated $800,000 in new business, what happened to your career track?

I was on the partner-track for the first time. I was up for a promotion to the next tier, which was a senior consultant. That was one of the job titles that led to becoming a partner.

• • •

How do you discern whether you're on the fast track or not?

If you are on it, you'll know it. You get the good assignments and the good projects. You have visibility, which means that the people who are higher up in the company pay some attention to you. They let you know that they like you. On projects and committees, you are asked for your opinion. You are brought along on higher-level sales calls and meetings. As a result, you are promoted quickly.

If you've wandered off the fast track onto a siding, you've got to admit it. I've seen it happen a lot of times, and it's usually because of something you did (or didn't do), and not what somebody else did to you. It is often hard to admit it.

EARNING MORE THAN YOUR MARKET

THE TRAP: You are paid much more than the current market for your position, which you consider to be a very fortunate situation, until you realize that you are priced out of the market.

THE LESSON: Early on in my executive search career, I met an accountant, whom we'll call Ted, who had worked for one of the largest public accounting firms. After his third year at the public accounting firm, he received a fantastic job offer, which resulted in him earning 40 percent more than anyone else of his experience level. Initially Ted was very excited, but after a few months that euphoria turned to frustration and then despair. He spent his days performing very routine accounting functions for a small company and, although he was very well paid, the opportunity for career advancement was nil. Nobody would hire him because he was making too much money for his experience.

Further, companies were reluctant to bring him on board with a pay cut when they could hire someone with similar experience who was paid according to the market and who would receive a nice salary increase. That person would be excited about the compensation as well as the job, whereas Ted would have to be stoic, to say the least, about taking a hefty pay cut in order to change jobs. While Ted knew he would have to take a lower salary in order to be competitive in the marketplace, he still resisted it emotionally.

THE TIP: Know your market and get paid in line with it—not over and not below. There are costs to making too much money.

I want to touch on another area that also comes into play when someone considers their market as they explore a new position and negotiate a job offer—stock options. You're one of the world's leading experts on employee stock options. Top executives such as a CEO hire consultants to help negotiate a stock options package. Someone making $100,000 to $200,000, however, isn't going to be able to do that. How can that person understand the world of stock options?

Let's start with the basics. A stock option gives a person the right to buy a share of stock at today's price any time over the next five to ten years. Let's say that the stock price today is $10 a share, and you have an option to buy stock for $10. In three years, let's say the stock is trading at $15 a share, and your option says you can buy it for $10. That's a pretty valuable opportunity. When a stock option is priced like that—you can buy the stock for less than where it's currently trading—your option is said to be "in the money." However, there is a risk to options because the stock price could also go down. In the example of the $10 stock option, in three years it's also possible that the stock could be trading at $8 or $5 a share, in which case your option isn't worth anything to you. It's called an "underwater" option because the market price is well below the option price.

• • •

Besides price, what else do I need to know about options so that I can understand what my company is giving me as a long-term incentive?

You need to know the terms of the options and how many of them you are getting. The term refers to the number of years you have to hold the options before they terminate or expire. Most options still have ten-year terms, although more have shorter terms of five to seven years. You also need to know the vesting schedule, which refers to how long before they become yours to exercise, which may range from one to five years. Options becoming vested and exercisable usually mean the same thing.

In addition, you would want to know what happens to your options should you leave the company. Do you get to keep them or do you have to give them up? Typically, unvested options are terminated and you cannot exercise them. The vested options that you hold must be exercised in thirty days, provided that they are "in the money."

• • •

How negotiable are stock options for someone in a midlevel position? What are the ground rules here?

It's probably easier to negotiate them than most people realize. In fact, it's probably easier to negotiate the number of options that you receive than it is to negotiate your salary—provided that you have an option-eligible position, of course. That eligibility, by the way, is usually defined and not negotiable.

Typically, companies define what job grades are eligible for receiving stock options. That doesn't mean that someone automatically receives them; rather, that person would be eligible. At higher job grades, a person is not only eligible but gets them every year. Eligibility for stock options could begin at salary levels as low as $60,000 to $80,000. If you are negotiating a six-figure salary job, there's a pretty good chance that you are eligible to receive options. This varies greatly between industries. In the technology field, it's almost guaranteed, while in banking you are much less likely to be option eligible.

• • •

Let's say that I'm negotiating a job offer that is option eligible. What is the right amount to ask for? If they offer me one amount, do I try to double it or ask for 25 percent more? What should I do?

First you ask, is this position eligible for options? If the answer is yes, then you ask, what is the range of possible option grants? You would also want to find out how many options the company grants on an annual basis. Now you are in a position to find out if it's possible to get a sign-on grant of stock options, the way you might get a sign-on bonus. You've got this nice moment in time as a job candidate when you are not on the annual salary and promotion grid. When you are being hired, your sign-on grant can come out of a different part of the company's budget, which means it's easier for the employer to give you a sign-on bonus and/or a sign-on option grant.

For example, you ask what the typical option grant is, and the company tells you 1,000 shares. Then you can ask for a sign-on option grant of, say, 3,000 shares. Asking for two or three times the annual grant upfront would not be inappropriate.

• • •

Are stock options the only kinds of incentives for which I might be eligible?

More and more frequently it's not just stock options grants. Companies are also giving restricted stock, which are full shares of stock that the company gives you but which you are restricted from selling or transferring to anyone else until those restrictions lapse.

Traps, Lessons, & Tips

STOCK OPTION NEGOTIATION: FIRST, YOU HAVE TO ASK

THE TRAP: You are not offered stock options or other long-term incentives as part of your compensation package; therefore you never bring it up in negotiation.

THE LESSON: It is perfectly acceptable in the course of your negotiations to inquire about the company's policies regarding stock options. If you are told that stock options are given to some employees, you can then ask what job levels are eligible for them. If the job you are pursuing is option eligible then by all means ask. You can also ask whether stock options can be part of your signing bonus. Discussions about how many stock options, vesting requirements (that is, when it's possible to "exercise" your options and convert them into stock), and all the rest can only occur after you ask.

THE TIP: You'll never know if you're eligible for stock options or if you could get more than you're offered initially, unless you ask.

What are the tax considerations for stock options and restricted stock?

Options have no tax consequences for you until you exercise them. Restricted stock is not taxable until it vests. Let's say the shares vest after three years; after that time you would be taxed on the full value of the stock. Sometimes companies also attach performance criteria to those grants, meaning that the company has to perform at a certain level or to a certain degree in order for those restricted shares to vest.

• • •

We've talked about the importance of knowing where a person is now in his or her current position in terms of job grade and salary level. We've also discussed understanding the competitive market by doing the necessary homework, researching salary levels, and doing some comparison shopping by going on several interviews. To further determine your market within a specific industry and at a particular company, what other factors should you consider?

Ask yourself: How does this company make money? You may be very good at what you do, but you are less likely to get promoted if you're not tied directly into how a company makes money. You want to be wired into the main juice of the organization. You'll know if you are: that's where the money is, where the responsibility and accountability are, and where the promotions are. You also need to know what creates value at the company, because the positions directly related to value creation will be the positions that will be most rewarded.

• • •

For example, in some corporate cultures, sales will be valued, while in others it will be product development or customer relationships. The questions to consider, therefore, are:

- How does this company make money?
- What does the company value?
- What is the value that I am creating?
- How does that fit into the company?

The answers to those questions will affect your initial compensation and your rate of compensation increases. If you're in a bank, for example, which makes money by loaning money and trading, but you're not involved in either of those activities, then you're outside the main flow. You may be in a position that serves that main flow, but you're still outside. A consulting firm makes money by selling services and delivering those services and projects to customers. The line partners are the ones who deliver on that.

You have to know where you are in the organization and whether or not you're in a place that's valued. If you are, then your market worth just went up.

The Compensation Structure

Salary negotiation takes place within a context that is governed by market conditions, influenced by the demand for people with your skills, your experience level, and even what part of the country you're in. That context is also set by the compensation structure of the company, whether it's large and bureaucratic or small and more loosely organized. As a skillful and confident negotiator of your next job offer, you have to be informed of the context in which you're working in order to get the most desirable outcome.

The place to start is with your current organization—or another organization if you are not currently employed. Learn everything you can about the job and compensation structure. In particular:

1. For your current position, is there a pay grade? What are the minimum, midpoint, and maximum for your grade? Where do you fall?
2. Map out the entire salary structure for your organization as well as you can, gathering as much data as you can, including pay grades, minimums, maximums, and midpoints.
3. Compare the highest-level individual contributor (nonmanager) with the lowest-level manager job grade, in terms of minimum, midpoint, and maximum salary levels.
4. What job levels in your organization are option eligible?
5. Using the Internet, professional associations, and any other resources you can find, obtain market information for your profession regarding as many aspects of compensation as you can find.
6. Are you currently underpaid, paid the right amount, or overpaid? Do the research to support your opinion.
7. At your organization, what are the functional areas that are directly related to how the company makes money. What job functions are considered to be most valuable? How valuable is your job function considered to be?

CHAPTER FIVE

Negotiating Salary with Your Current Employer

You've been at your job for a while, and you've proven yourself. Every year, more responsibilities have been added to your job, although your title remains the same. You know this occurs frequently with employees who are seen as high performers: when something needs to get done, managers give the task to their best people. With all that's been added to your job, you have more responsibility and are performing better than your peers. There was no singular event that caused this disparity. You weren't promoted, per se. It just happened because you do more (and better), and more is asked and expected of you.

Now it's time to revisit your salary.

Or, perhaps you've been with the company less than year. However, when you first took the job—which involved a substantial pay cut—you negotiated when your first salary review would be. (As stated in Chapter 6, one of the things often overlooked in job negotiations is the fact that your first salary review may be negotiable.) You accepted the pay cut because you wanted to change fields and to prove yourself in a different type of job. So when you accepted the job you told your hiring manager: "I'll take the salary you're offering me now. Just give me six months to prove myself. After that, review my performance, and pay me what you think I'm worth."

Now the time has come to talk salary.

In this chapter, I'm going to address some important questions regarding how to approach salary negotiations with your current employer and the strategies that will make this a positive and fruitful experience for both sides.

First, there are ground rules to keep in mind when you are negotiating salary with your current employer. Remember (as stated in Chapter 10), it is a sales process—in which you want to be a buyer, even though you are also a seller at times. As part of this process, you are "selling" to your employer your features and benefits: who you are; what you've done for them; and what you are going to do for them in the future. The more benefits you offer them, the higher your compensation should be.

Benefits, however, exist in the mind of the beholder. In other words, what *you* think is a benefit and what *your boss* thinks is a benefit may not be the same thing. For that reason, you must be sure to be on the same wavelength as your boss with regard to what is valued in your company, the corporate culture, and the priorities that have been established in the organization.

Here's an analogous example to illustrate the point: I was being sold a telephone system for my company. The salesperson kept going on and on about this feature and that feature of the phone system—almost none of which I thought I would ever use. As a result, I would not consider the phone system. I believed that it must be overpriced for what I needed because it had all these features that I wasn't going to use. What the salesperson saw as benefits, I perceived as detriments.

Drawing from this example, what the employee must do in salary negotiation with his current employer is demonstrate the benefits he has that the employer also values.

One of the big advantages of negotiating with your current employer, versus a new employer, is that (presumably) you know what the priorities are and you know what's important to the organization. You know what the problems are, you know the objectives, and you know your boss's hot buttons.

Going back to the example of the telephone system, what the salesperson should have done was find out exactly what features I wanted and then demonstrated to me that the phone system would do exactly what I needed, how the system would help me now and continue to serve me and my company in the future. All of those features that the phone system had, which were beyond my present and future needs, were irrelevant, and by focusing on them, the salesperson undermined the sale.

Similarly, your job in maximizing your compensation will be based on how well you communicate and demonstrate to your manager the benefits that you bring and the contribution that you will be capable of making in the future.

There are some advantages of negotiating with an existing company that you probably don't have with a new employer. When you are a new or prospective employee, you may only have one or two sources of information. When you have been working at a company for some time, however, you have access to much more information about the organization and its practices. For example, if you've been with the company for a while, you have friends within the organization, and your friends have friends. This allows you to find out more about the culture and what's possible in terms of compensation. One of the critical questions that people need to know—and this applies in their current company as well as a new company—is *what is possible*. What is negotiable: another week of vacation, or more bonus potential? What is the maximum salary you can get? On what basis are these decisions made? If you move to a different city, will your salary increase? Many companies have policies that relate salary to the cost of living in a particular location, while others do not. What is your organization's policy regarding location?

Negotiating with your existing employer is also a different dynamic from dealing with a new or prospective employer. In a new company, if you ask for too much money, it could end the opportunity. In your current job, if you ask for too much money, the company isn't going to terminate you. One thing to keep in mind, though: By asking for too much money in your current job, you may be signaling—perhaps unintentionally—that you are quite unhappy in your current situation or looking for a new position. *Everything you do affects the company's perception of you. There is no neutral.*

There are also disadvantages of negotiating with your existing company. One is that you have less leverage. If a prospective employer offers you something you don't want and you say no, the company won't get your services. With your current employer, if you say no, the company still gets your services (at least for now). Your current employer probably realizes that most people are reluctant to willingly enter the job search process. For most people, looking for a job is a difficult, time-consuming, and stressful experience. How willing are you going to be to put yourself through the job search just to raise your salary? There has been much research over the past forty years that shows compensation is not a satisfier, although it is a dissatisfier. If you are unhappy in your job, getting paid more money will not make you happy. However, if you are happy in your job but you are underpaid, that *will* make you unhappy.

PAY ME MORE OR I'M OUTTA HERE!

THE TRAP: You accept a counteroffer from your current company in order to increase your salary.

THE LESSON: Amanda was unhappy with her pay at her current job, so she pursued a position with a competitor and negotiated an offer with a higher salary. When her current employer made a counteroffer with a considerable increase in her salary, she accepted, as that was what Amanda had hoped would happen all along. A year later when her company had a round of layoffs because of changing market conditions, Amanda was one of the first to be let go because she was overpaid compared to her performance. The other opportunity at the competitor firm was no longer available.

THE TIP: If you want more money from your current employer, negotiate based on your value contribution, rather than using a threat.

Knowing when to bring up the salary discussion and with whom is a matter of discernment, and it is situational. You can't just waltz into the boss's office one day and say, "Hey, I think I deserve a raise."

In some cases you'll be discussing salary with your current manager because of a change in your responsibilities, and in others you'll be talking to a new hiring manager within the company because you're up for a promotion.

Let's consider some examples: You are a sales rep, reporting to a district manager, who in turn reports to a regional manager. The company approaches you about becoming a district manager.

As we'll discuss later in this chapter, the appropriate business protocol in this situation is to talk about the career opportunity *first* to see if it is of interest to you and a fit with your desired career path. Once you've established that this opportunity would be good for you, it would be appropriate to ask, "What are you thinking about compensation for me?" One thing to keep in mind, however: If your initial discussion about the promotion takes place with your current manager and not the manager of the new position, it may not be the right time to mention compensation at all. That discussion should happen with the actual hiring manager of the new position.

Using another example, let's say that you've grown in your current position and have additional duties and broader responsibilities. Your salary, however, has not reflected the job change. One obvious time for this discussion is when (and if) your company has a formal salary review, which is often concurrent with the performance review. So that's another element to consider: Is your salary review part of the same process as your performance review, or is it done at a different time? In some companies, salary review occurs after the formal performance review is concluded so that review data can be included in the compensation discussion.

As a boss, I was open to people coming to me and asking for a raise in salary so long as they could justify the request. An administrative assistant at my former company came to me and explained that since she was hired she had been taking on more responsibilities with clients and doing a much bigger job, and therefore she deserved a raise. She was right! Her contribution was real, and I increased her salary to reflect the contribution she was making.

Seeking Rewards for a Big Success

Another time your salary might be raised is when you have scored a big success that has resulted in a substantial financial gain for your company. You sold $30 million in business that resulted in $5 million in profit for the company. You created a new product, or you streamlined operations that resulted in significant savings. Normally, this type of accomplishment would be discussed as part of your normal review. But let's say that reviews are not done on a regular basis and/or the contribution that you've made to your company is really extraordinary. (Much would depend upon the culture of your company; in some firms it would be completely inappropriate to go to your boss and ask for a raise in salary because of such a win. Instead, you'd wait until your next review. This type of conversation is more common in smaller companies where reviews tend to be more informal.) Assuming that you feel confident that having a conversation with your boss would be in keeping with your corporate culture, and your success warrants it, you could go to your boss and say, "I think I've really increased my contribution to the company. I'd like an increase in my salary or a bonus for what I've accomplished."

Whether salary review is part of your performance review or conducted separately, you must keep in mind that one big influencer in your manager's decision of how much you should be paid is how much he appreciates you. The reality is people are paid more when they are appreciated by their managers, their managers' managers, and on up the line.

It may be surprising, and maybe a little disturbing, to know that how well you're liked is part of the compensation equation. Most people assume that pay is reflective only of their performance. This then raises the question: What else goes on in the minds of managers and employers when it comes to deciding how much people are paid.

In general, managers take some key questions under consideration when they think about how much to pay someone:

- How well does this person perform?
- Is he currently at the right pay level, overpaid, or underpaid compared with his peers and the market?
- Is she is in a key position in the company? Do we really want to keep her?
- How well does he fit with our company and our culture?
- Is she happy here?
- Are we in danger of losing him? Is he the type of person who may be actively recruited by our competitors?
- Is she so unhappy that she'll actively look for another position?

- Do we like her? Do I like her?
- How important is it for us to keep him?
- What is her future with the organization? How far up in the organization might she go?
- Is he one of our top performers?

This last question—whether or not you are a top performer— really carries a lot of weight. A person who is perceived to be a top-performer will be well rewarded, even if he isn't liked all that much. That person will be well paid, although perhaps not promoted. However, being well liked will go a long way toward making a manager more willing to at least consider a pay increase for you.

Understand that some of these questions may be asked consciously, and others will not. Nonetheless, these considerations are still, to some degree, part of managers' gut-level, unconscious decision-making process.

Getting Feedback on How People Feel about You

Since perception is so critical, it's essential to know how people really feel about you. One of the most important tactics employees can use to succeed is to understand how their managers and other leaders perceive them. How much feedback a person receives, however, has a lot to do with them. In fact, many employees are very effective at training their managers not to give them feedback. So if you *don't* want to be given any kind of feedback, here's what you should do:

- When you are given any kind of feedback about what you've done or how you've interacted with others, immediately explain that the person giving you feedback is wrong.
- When you are given feedback about something or receive any kind of criticism about what you've done, make excuses and justify your actions.

- Point the finger at other people and explain how it is their fault and not yours.

- Communicate in as many ways as you can how much you don't want to receive feedback—in other words, make them pay for having given it to you.

As an employer, I can tell you that dealing with someone who is defensive when it comes to feedback is not only irritating, but it also tells a lot about the person's abilities (or lack thereof). Here's a story of my experience with a young man I hired several years ago at my search firm.

The young man, whom we'll call Paul, was hired to recruit accountants. As such, part of his job was to call managers at accounting firms and find out what their employee placement needs were. Partly because of his youth and inexperience, Paul addressed every manager he talked to as "Mr. Smith" or "Ms. Jones." I knew that his deferential air was also due to upbringing and lack of experience. So on his second day on the job, I gave him a little feedback: "Paul, I understand that you want to be polite and show respect because you're dealing with people who are older than you, but it doesn't work in this business to call everyone 'Mr.' and 'Ms.' You have to address them by their first names."

Paul's response? He went on to explain, at length, why he was doing that—and why it was the right thing to do. What was going on in my head while he gave his "explanation" in response to my feedback? I was thinking: Why would anybody on his second day on the job in a new career that he knows nothing about explain to me—who owns the company and is considered a highly successful expert in the business—why he's doing something that I told him not to do? Why would he try to prove that he did the right thing after I just finished explaining it wouldn't work?

Paul lasted two weeks on the job.

While this is an extreme example, I can cite countless others of managers who stopped giving feedback to employees because it was painful to do so. Giving feedback is hard enough for most people, and when they hit a brick wall of resistance on the part of the other person, it's even more painful.

We all know (or at least we say we do) that feedback is important. But it goes beyond the obvious points of what you're doing well and what you're doing not so well. All feedback from the leaders in your organization is incredibly helpful to any employee who wants to succeed. Feedback tells you what's important to the leaders, what's critical to the organization, and what matters. It tells you how you are being perceived in relation to what's important. It tells you where your perceived deficits lie. Feedback will let you know if you need to do more of something, and what you need to do differently. You'll also find out if what you do well is less important to the organization.

If you are a relatively new employee, feedback gives you invaluable data about what the organization values and what its priorities are. To illustrate, let's use a concrete example. Some organizations are very process oriented; others are much more results oriented. A process-oriented organization greatly values operating in accordance with established procedures and within specific channels. A results-oriented culture may not care whether you use set procedures and channels; it cares much more about the results that are obtained.

The same person who performs well in those two different cultures will receive different feedback based on what the organization values. In a process-oriented culture, the person will be told: "Good job. We like the way you work within the organization, and we like the way you work with people." In a results-oriented organization, the feedback received will be: "Great. You got the job done." The culture shapes the nature of the feedback, even given the exact same performance and the same person doing the work. That feedback, in turn, provides a tremendous amount of information about the respective culture. In fact, feedback tells you as much about the organization and the person giving you the feedback as it does about your behavior and performance.

Direct vs. Indirect Communication

Another distinction in corporate cultures is whether communication tends to be direct or indirect. In a culture of indirect communication, people are generally afraid to say what they really think. For example, if the boss says something that people disagree with, they will not say so directly. When disagreements aren't expressed directly, employees will tend to express them in more indirect and often more damaging ways. For example, the manager asks you to do something within a time frame that you do not think is reasonable. Rather than say, "I can't complete that task in that time frame," you agree to the assignment, then drag your feet and make excuses for why it can't be done—then justify not getting it done. In a culture that values direct communication, you would be far more apt to say: "I can't see how I can accomplish that task in the time frame you've suggested. These are the obstacles I see to getting it accomplished." You and your manager would engage in some meaningful problem solving, either to overcome those obstacles or to change the timeline to accomplish the objective.

Here's another example of direct versus indirect communication. You are asked to give your opinion regarding someone who is up for a promotion. You don't think this is a good idea, but in a culture that uses indirect communication you wouldn't say anything because you don't want to rock the boat. You want to avoid conflict, so you keep quiet. However, you're still opposed to the promotion, so you don't support that person. As a result, the person fails, and everyone loses.

In many companies, feedback seems hard to come by. Everyone—especially managers—is busy getting the work done, and the workload is used as an excuse not to give substantive feedback. Someone might occasionally get an e-mail that says, "Thanks for your work on the project" or "Good job," or maybe a few lines of advice or correction. As a result, most of the time feedback is hard to come by. This puts the onus on you to make sure you're getting the feedback you need to make sure you're on track and to open the door to negotiating your next salary increase.

Performance Reviews

If you have an effective performance management process, you should be getting feedback at least as part of your annual review. However, few managers have been trained to give feedback, and most do a poor job of it. It is your job as an employee to get that feedback. In the performance-review process, the most obvious thing to do is make sure that you have a sit-down meeting with your manager. At most large companies this is a prescribed part of the process, but frequently it doesn't occur or it only occurs in a perfunctory manner. *It is your job to make it meaningful.* Here are some questions you can ask to facilitate this process: What do you think that I do well? What would you like me to do better? What areas and/or skills do you think I need to improve? If you were me, and you wanted to be as successful as possible here, what would you do? What do you think my career potential is in this company? What other advice do you have for me?

Your objective in this process is to show whoever is giving you the feedback that you are grateful that they took the time to give it to you. The more critical the feedback, the more gratitude you need to express. They are giving you a gift with their feedback—no matter what it is. Your job is to express thanks for that gift. If you do, you'll be more likely to receive more "gifts"—that is, more feedback.

Sometimes feedback is tough to hear. We love it when somebody is telling us how great we are or how well we did something, but we cringe at the thought of criticism, whether constructive or not. Still, wouldn't you rather know so that you can do something about it?

Let's take a simple example: Imagine that you have bad breath. Would you rather go around all day with bad breath and have no one tell you—even though everyone is put off by you? Or would you rather have the first person you see in the day tell you, which will most likely be an embarrassing encounter for both of you? Obviously, you'd want to be told immediately so you could correct it! Now take this example and expand it into other areas: Let's say you spoke too harshly to a subordinate. You didn't understand the implications of what your manager said to you. You spoke too much and didn't listen well in a meeting. You were late for a meeting. You don't respond to e-mails in a timely manner. You spend too much time on low-priority tasks. Wouldn't you rather be told as soon as possible so that you can take corrective action?

Remember, a performance review is only one day out of approximately 250 workdays a year when you formally receive feedback. You can also receive it moment-by-moment from just about anyone, including subordinates or direct reports, peers, managers and leaders, peers and colleagues, and customers—both internal and external.

Starting the Salary Conversation

Once someone has received feedback and understands what's important to the company given its culture, it's time to start the salary conversation. There are several steps to the salary negotiation process. As mentioned earlier in this chapter, you need to know and be able to communicate how you have benefited your organization and your manager in the past. Managers come in all flavors and management styles. A significant percentage of managers don't even know how well their subordinates have performed. The truth is many managers will not be adequately prepared for the salary review process. They will not have done their homework. In any case, it's your job to be fully prepared.

Being fully prepared has three elements: One is to understand your company's culture and policies regarding compensation. The second is to document as fully as possible what you have done and what you have accomplished, as well as how competent you are. Third, you must develop the optimal relationships within the organization so that the decision-makers are inclined to treat you well.

When it comes to compensation, companies are all over the place, with a wide range of policies, procedures, and cultures. Some companies have no formal review process, and people only get raises when their managers feel like it. Other companies have formal processes such as annual reviews that are frequently ignored, and people can go eighteen months to two years without a review. For many companies, the process is formal and followed throughout the organization. Generally large companies are more formal and consistent in practice than smaller companies. In large companies, the salary review process is typically tied to an annual performance review cycle, in which managers formally assess their subordinates and direct reports. In smaller companies, there may or may not be a performance review process, and salary determination may be totally off-the-cuff.

Another important element to understand in your organization's culture in relation to compensation is how pay is structured. Some companies have very formal pay systems with a range that has a bottom, top, and midpoint. Other companies have broad pay bands that a number of jobs fall into, and those bands have upper, lower, and midpoint numbers. Other companies are much more informal and have more flexibility.

At some companies, it is easy to obtain compensation policy, while at others the practice is not to reveal this information to employees. You should find out as much as you can about your organization's compensation practices. Contact human resources. Ask your manager (although she may not know much more than you do). Talk to your friends around the coffee machine. Notice who is paid well and why. Who was promoted, and why was that person promoted? Was it her outstanding performance, or had he developed relationships within the organization? Did she succeed in completing an outstanding project? These things all give you important insight into what is rewarded and what you should be doing within the company.

Letting Your Boss Know What You've Done

In the salary review process, two different kinds of things are measured. One is your accomplishments and results, which is what you've done. The second is the competencies, traits, or standards (which may be called a number of different things), which is how you've done your job. This is analogous to your first-grade report card, when you were given one grade that showed how well you did on the subject matter and another grade that measured how well you participated in class.

Your preparation for the negotiation should include both the "what" and the "how." The what for you is your accomplishments, both as an individual and in a group or team. Document as much as you can. If you developed a new procedures manual, write it down and bring it with you to the review. In the world of art, people carry around a big portfolio that shows their work. When it comes time for your review, you should do the same thing.

One of the techniques for doing this is to keep a journal. Keep track of affirmations and the appreciation—the e-mails and the notes from customers and others—that you've received. If you received something verbally, write the comment down, whom you received it from, and when. Details are important.

For some people keeping track of all the praise they've received and sharing it with their bosses is difficult. They may be reluctant to do so because they believe that would be boasting or "tooting their own horn." Based on their personal, family, cultural, and/or religious background, they feel that it is wrong to "brag" or tell people how good they are. They may think that talking about what they've accomplished is selfish, rude, or self-aggrandizing. That's not the case at all. You certainly want to communicate your accomplishments and successes in a manner that's culturally acceptable for your organization. But how are you going to be appreciated, valued, and fairly compensated if people don't know what you've done? If you have received some positive feedback from a customer, for example, it reflects well on both you and the whole organization—so tell your boss.

When You're Up for a Promotion

When the subject of a promotion comes up, you also need to know how to negotiate a raise that is fair to both sides. The underlying question here is, what is the relationship between promotion and pay? Companies are different in their policies regarding the issue. My advice, in general, is to keep the discussions of promotion and pay separate but related. When a promotion comes up, if you want it, go after it. You don't have to wait until performance review time to have the promotion discussion. If you have ambition for a different position, find the best time to express it to your manager and to other appropriate people.

Here are two different scenarios regarding promotion. The first is the company approaches you to see if you are interested in a job change, and the second is you take the initiative to pursue a promotion or job change within the company. If the company comes to you, then as you do your information-gathering about the job, there are certain, essential things that you must find out, such as what the job entails, who reports to you, and to whom you will report. One of your *last* questions should be about the compensation for the job. It is important that this be one of the last questions you ask—instead of one of the first—so that you're not perceived only as money-motivated. You want to show that you are looking at factors such as your career path, the opportunity to be challenged, learn new things, and make a more important contribution to the company, and so forth. Managers do not trust that people will remain motivated and committed to doing a great job if all they care about is the money.

In the second scenario, in which you find out about an opportunity and you approach your manager or another company leader about it, it's even more important that the salary negotiation occur later in the conversation. Your primary objective in this instance is to sell the company on your desire to do the job and your ability to handle the responsibilities.

When Money Is the Motivating Factor

There may be times or situations, however, when your motivating factor really *is* making more money. Let's say you love your job: what you do, the people you work with, everything about it. But you have a change in life circumstances—the pending birth of twins or having three kids in college, for example. There are ways, however, to approach your boss and be honest about your need to make more money. For example, there are times and situations when it would be appropriate to go to your employer and say, "I need to make more money because of this circumstance. How can I do that?"

Your goal is to engage your manager in discussions on how you can maximize your contribution to the organization and be compensated for it. However, pay follows performance, not the personal situation. Few managers will pay you more just because you have a change in circumstances. They are going to pay you more money because they value you and your contribution and consider you worthy of the compensation they pay you.

WHEN YOU NEED TO MAKE MORE MONEY

THE TRAP: You tell your boss that you need to make more money because you bought a bigger house, you have two kids in college, you need a new car, etc.

THE LESSON: When you need to make more money, figure out how you can contribute more. Consider saying to your manager, "I need to make more money. What contribution can I make so that you would think it fair to pay me more?" Or if you think you are already contributing significantly more, then make the case to your boss.

THE TIP: To get paid more, demonstrate the increased value that you can contribute or are already contributing.

It's important to understand what goes through the employer's (or manager's) mind when people say they need to make more money. As an employer, I've had experiences at both ends of the spectrum: top-performing individuals who sold me on their ability to do another job or take on more responsibility that would justify them earning more money, as well as people who weren't doing their current jobs that well. When someone who has not been particularly successful in her current position now says that she needs more money, what goes on in my head is: You've got to be kidding! You haven't performed here for the amount of money you are making, so why would I believe that you will perform better for more money? You're not making me happy now. I have made the mistake of believing people will perform better when they are paid more, and it never worked.

Here's one example where someone did need to make more money, and management was willing to take a chance on him because of his positive track record. The person was a successful engineer but due to family circumstances needed to make more money. He approached his manager and the HR department to open discussions. Because of the company's compensation policies and the fact that he was already paid at the top end of the salary range, his salary goal could not be reached in his current position.

As he looked around the company, however, the engineer saw that his outgoing personality and his experience interfacing with the sales team in a product-support capacity made him a good candidate for a sales job. Given his proven track record as an engineer, he was considered a viable candidate. He began discussions with management about moving him into a sales role. It was a risk to both sides, but the positives outweighed the negatives, so they decided to give it a try.

What's going on in the manager's head during these discussions? I like him. He has delivered and performed for me and the organization. I want him to do well. I want him to stay with the company and have his needs met. I don't know for certain if he can do this new job, but I'm hopeful, and he has earned the chance to prove himself.

The Risk of Getting Another Offer

Trying to increase your salary with your current employer by getting a job offer from a competitor or someone outside the industry is a risky strategy. The outcome you're hoping for is to get a counteroffer from your current employer that at least matches or exceeds the offer from the other company. On the face of it, it would appear to be an effective strategy. If the outside employer offers you, say, a 20 percent increase and your company matches it, you'll likely make far more than you would if you continued on your typical performance/salary review path. If you are going to employ this strategy, however, you should be aware of the risks.

First, realize what message you are sending to your current employer—where you have decided to continue working. Your employer no longer sees you as a trusted or loyal employee. Your manager is thinking, I cannot count on you to be here longer. If you stay, there is a risk that you will be working for the competition in the future. I can't trust you because the likelihood of you leaving is high. You don't really want to be here because if you did, you wouldn't have been out in the job market. And if you were so unhappy here, why didn't you come talk to me about it?

If you do decide to accept the counteroffer and stay with your current employer, it is critically important that you communicate the following: I love working here at this organization. I like you as my manager, and I want to work for you.

Even with a lucrative counteroffer, employees usually do not stay for very long. Research shows that most people who accept a counteroffer are gone within a year or two. Often the circumstances surrounding their leaving are less advantageous than the offer that they received. Why? Because something prompted that employee in the first place to pursue another job opportunity. Even though the employee has received a counteroffer and agreed to stay, whatever made the employee dissatisfied, restless, or long for a new challenge is still there. Even with more money, the employee won't be any happier in his old job.

The moral of this story: Do not pursue an outside offer if your only intent is to make your current employer pay you more money. If you do receive an offer for a new job that genuinely interests you, be very wary about accepting a counteroffer to stay at your current job.

There are exceptions, of course. Someone I know very well wanted to change fields within his profession, which prompted him to look for another job with a different employer. His current employer, however, recognized his value as an employee and wanted him to stay on. The counteroffer that he ended up accepting from his current employer allowed him to change his career direction, make a contribution in a new area, and gain valuable experience in the process. After two years, he migrated into a new position in his new field. Now, ten years later, he is a successful entrepreneur in this field.

This type of scenario is the exception and not the norm. If the manager is prepared to make the employee a counteroffer, he's probably thinking something like: The next time, this person will leave on my terms. She is in a critical job that I need filled with an experienced person. I can't afford to have her leave me in the lurch. I will make her a counteroffer then take the next year or however long it takes to groom someone else for that position. I will have a succession plan in place. That way, when she leaves, as she probably will, I'll be prepared. Once I have someone in place, I might encourage her to seek another opportunity somewhere else. I will make something happen.

Successful Negotiations with Your Current Employer

Negotiating salary with your current employer requires preparation on your part. It's your job to know what the company values, its expectations and objectives, and the culture of the organization. Given that information, you need to demonstrate how you have met those demands, made a valuable contribution, and what you will do in the future. In order to gather this strategic information, you must seek out and welcome feedback, particularly from your boss. Don't be afraid to ask what you need to improve upon or the areas that your boss would like to see you develop. Feedback will not only give you insight into how your performance is perceived, but you'll also learn what is important to your boss and your boss's boss.

The opportunity to discuss salary may come up as part of a formal performance and/or salary review process, or you may have to request a sit-down meeting with your boss. At all times, remember that pay follows performance. No one is going to pay you more money simply because you've asked. Once you've demonstrated what you have done and can do, let your boss know what more you can take on. In most organizations, the more you do, the more responsibilities you'll be given. The bigger your contribution, the more valuable you are. The greater your value, the stronger your case will be for an increase in pay.

Building Your Case for a Raise

As a successful salary negotiator, you need to build your case for getting more money—not because you want it, but because your performance and your contribution to the company warrant it.

The purpose of the following exercise is to help you build your case for performance reviews and to prepare for the next conversation you have with your manager about your performance, your responsibilities and how they've grown, and the pay you deserve. Write down your answers in a journal that you update continually. Here are some suggestions:

- What was your most significant accomplishment over the past week?
- What were your top three accomplishments over the last month?
- What were ten of your most significant accomplishments over the last year?
- Why do you deserve to be promoted?
- When do you think you will be ready for a promotion?
- When employees are promoted in your organization, what are the main reasons? A successful project? Strong relationships with management? A long-term track record of success?
- What is your strategy for promotion?
- What are your organization's policies and practices regarding salary increases? Is there a standard annual cost-of-living increase? Do employees in different locations receive different compensation based on cost of living? On what basis are bonuses paid?

CHAPTER SIX

Your Benefits Package

with Tom Terry

When it comes to a total compensation package, benefits is an area about which employees know little. For example, many midlevel employees and managers don't know how much leverage they may have to negotiate aspects of their benefits package, such as extra vacation or an accelerated vesting in the new employer's 401(k) plan.

For Dave Jensen, benefits—such as health coverage, vacation, and the company's 401(k)—did not come up until the end of the job negotiation process. At that point, he was given a summary sheet of the company's benefits, which he admits he didn't even read. "I figured it was pretty standard with any other company. I made a lot of assumptions about benefits, some of which turned out to be wrong. For example, I figured they'd offer a pretty competitive health package, but it turns out I'm paying more now than I was in my last job," Dave says. "I didn't even ask what premium I would be paying. I thought maybe I wasn't supposed to ask those questions, that if I did I might offend the company and jeopardize my chance of getting the job."

His focus, he reiterates, was on the salary, which was the top concern for him throughout the process. What he didn't know, however, was that since his starting salary was less than what he had been making, he could negotiate to be "made whole" in other areas such as with more vacation time. "I didn't try to negotiate on vacation," he says. "I didn't know that I could do that."

Before job seekers open the discussion regarding the benefits that the company is offering, there are a few ground rules to understand:

- The higher up the corporate ladder someone is, the more flexibility there will be, in general, in negotiating benefits. Lower-level employees have virtually no leverage when it comes to making special requests in their benefits, although there are questions that every employee should ask, such as whether a pre-existing medical condition would be immediately covered by the hiring company's medical plan. For midlevel employees receiving a high five-figure or low six-figure salary, there may be more room to ask for enhanced benefits, if they know what—and how—to ask.

- Understanding your current and future benefits packages requires that you do your homework. It's not easy to place a value on your health benefits, sick leave, and vacation pay. But there are tools available that give you a place to start. Once you know what you're already receiving, you'll be in a better position to analyze the benefits that are being offered to you—and what you might be gaining or losing.

In this chapter, Tom Terry, a career benefits expert and founder of CCA Strategies, a leading actuarial consulting firm, discusses the ins and outs of several benefits issues. His firm provides compensation and employee benefits consulting for a wide variety of employers, including some of the largest companies. The purpose of his company, Tom explains, is to "bring clarity where complexity is the rule" and to help employers make better and more-informed decisions about benefit plans in order to deploy their human resources dollars in the most effective way possible.

As the CEO of the firm that he founded and as an employer, he has expertise in an area which many job seekers fail to research adequately. He offers valuable advice on what you should know about your current and future benefits packages and suggestions on how to evaluate and negotiate a package as part of the best possible job offer for you and your situation.

•　　•　　•

Most people don't think of benefits as being part of their compensation. They regard such things as vacation or health insurance as some standard offering that the company gives. Can you give us a brief look at the history of benefits?

The first thing to understand is that benefits are a form of tax-free or tax-deferred compensation, with a favored tax status under the law. Health-care benefits, for example, can be given to employees tax-free. One caveat is that employers have to distribute these benefits across the board; the government doesn't want this type of tax-free compensation skewed toward highly compensated employees.

Benefits became prevalent after World War II when postwar inflation and wage controls enacted by Congress created the need for a new type of compensation that would reduce taxable wages. The 1950s also saw the rise of labor unions that were able to successfully negotiate significant improvements in employee benefits for rank-and-file employees. Once companies gave these benefits to their hourly employees, they began distributing them to salaried employees as well.

In general, particularly from a big-company perspective, benefits are a "welfare system," a way for the employer to take care of employees. Benefits packages for the rank-and-file tend to be one-size-fits-all, with the company offering employees the same health plans, paid sick leave, vacation policy, and retirement policies. In the upper levels of the hierarchy pyramid, however, benefits that are doled out to the masses do not serve the needs of the marketplace when an employer is trying to attract a higher-level executive. In this instance, benefits are highly negotiable.

● ● ●

Understanding that benefits are part of compensation helps to clarify the issue in employees' minds that they can, to some degree, negotiate the package they receive. What's the first thing to understand about negotiating benefits?

The moment you raise the issue and the company is being asked to do something "special" for midlevel professionals in terms of benefits, there will be pushback. When a midlevel executive makes a request for some change or addition to benefits, the most likely response from human resources or the benefits department will be "we can't do that." They communicate that there are firm limits to what can be granted. As far as they are concerned, there is no way on earth they are going to give something special to anyone. In the executive ranks, companies frequently make exceptions when it comes to benefits, but for everyone else, there will be great resistance to do anything special.

● ● ●

So is it that they can't do anything, or that they won't do anything?

That's exactly the point: They say "can't," but usually they really mean "won't." Let's look at the dynamics involved. As I stated before, if someone is coming in as a top-level executive, there is the general assumption among all parties that benefits are at least somewhat negotiable. One commonly negotiated area is "recognition of past service," which applies to retirement plans and even medical coverage. Some companies also have vacation plans that are tied to length of service: e.g., two weeks of vacation the first year, three weeks after five years, and four weeks after ten years. At the executive level, years of past service are commonly taken into consideration for the purpose of benefits. This is also often taken into account for middle managers and employees in an area such as vacation time.

• • •

Let's start there. Say I'm a midlevel executive, and I've been recruited by a company that's offering me a low six-figure salary. In my previous job, I had three weeks of vacation. The benefits department in the new company, however, informs me that, according to company policy, I will only receive two weeks of vacation. I won't get three weeks until after five years. Can I negotiate with my new employer to continue receiving three weeks of vacation?

Vacation is one area in which companies have the most freedom. Extra vacation is like "hidden money" that the human resources or benefits department can give out without anyone being held accountable. Vacation is largely an unregulated benefit because it's just pay continuation while someone is off work. So if you're being heavily recruited for a position and you tell human resources that you've had three weeks of vacation at your previous employer, you can make a good case to receive additional vacation in the new job. The key concept here is that you want your previous experience to be recognized.

Here's the rationale: The new employer is recruiting you because of your experience. Shouldn't this experience be taken into consideration for your benefits as well? If the company won't budge, and you're a highly sought-after individual, there is the risk that you could go somewhere else to work. The more competitive the situation and the more heavily recruited someone is, the better the chance of having past experience recognized. In the area of vacation, this is probably one of the easiest areas in which to be "made whole" in terms of what the employee received from a previous employer.

WHEN YOU DON'T ASK, YOU USUALLY DON'T GET

THE TRAP: You don't ask for more benefits because you think the package can't be changed.

THE LESSON: Frederico had five weeks of vacation at his current position. When he was offered a job with an increase in pay at another company, he was told that the company's policy was two weeks of vacation for the first five years. He approached his hiring manager and told him that this was a deal breaker. The manager, a long-term employee who knew the ropes, went to the head of HR and got approval to match his five weeks of vacation. Frederico accepted the offer.

THE TIP: Don't assume that benefits are cast in stone until you ask.

Besides vacation time, what else could a midlevel employee or manager negotiate in order to have past experience recognized?

With other benefits it gets more complicated. Take the area of pensions and retirement plans. Here there are more hard-dollars involved. It is possible to negotiate recognition of previous experience in order to be immediately vested (or vested very soon) in the company's portion of contributions made to a 401(k) plan. Typically vesting takes place over five years. (Vesting in this instance refers to the employee's right to the company's contribution to a retirement plan. The employee's own contribution in pretax dollars is not subject to any vesting requirements. Whatever the employee puts in, he/she would be entitled to—even if that person leaves after a year.)

•   •   •

If you're a midlevel employee or manager, what would be the best way to approach the topic of accelerated vesting as part of negotiating your job offer?

The best way to approach this is with the assumption that you are going to be made whole in terms of your benefits. Here's what I mean. Let's say you are already employed, and a competing company is trying to hire you away from your current employer. In this instance, you are in a very good position compared with someone who is among a thousand applicants for a job! In a competitive situation, you are going to start with the assumption that you will be made whole in your benefits; you're not going to lose anything. If you had four weeks of vacation, and you were fully vested in your retirement plan at your current employer, you will expect the same level of benefits from the new employer.

• • •

What are the ways in which an employee can be made whole in a situation such as you describe?

There are basically two tracks: One is by making the benefits as identical as possible—for example, by agreeing to accelerated vesting. The other is to make up for what is lost through a signing bonus. Let's say that if you leave Company A, you will lose "X" value in benefits if you go to work for Company B. Perhaps you're just a year away from being fully vested in your 401(k) plan, and you know how much of the company's contribution you stand to lose. One way to compensate for that loss is with a signing bonus, which is "grossed up" for taxes (meaning that the amount you receive after taxes is equal to the value of the lost benefits.) The same could apply for a loss in the value of medical benefits.

• • •

In a few instances, it's fairly easy to calculate what you stand to lose. For example, if you're only 50 percent or 80 percent vested in the company's contribution to your 401(k) plan, those numbers are readily available on your 401(k) statement. If the company's contribution to date is $10,000 and you're 80 percent vested, you'll take $8,000 of the company's money with you when you leave. The other 20 percent, or $2,000, is what you're losing by changing jobs. But what about other benefits? How can you compare, for example, the value of a health plan at one company versus another?

There are online tools that can help you (for example, the University of California at Riverside offers this calculator: *http://atyourservice .ucop.edu/applications/total_comp/index.php*).

Even a simple grid or spreadsheet can help you look at what benefits you are currently receiving and what the new company is offering. Here's a very basic example:

TABLE FOUR

EVALUATING YOUR BENEFITS

	Current Position	New Position
Vacation	3 weeks	2 weeks to start; 3 weeks after 5 years
Medical		
Premium I must pay:	$225/month	$275/month
Deductible (in network):	$750	$1,000
Deductible (out of network):	$2,500	$3,000
Dental		
Premium I must pay:	$50/month	$55/month
401(k):		
Company Contribution:	Matches up to 10% of my contribution	Matches up to 8% of employee contribution
Current vesting:	Fully vested	Fully vested after 5 years

• • •

Even in a simple comparison like this, things may not match up all nice and even, with one company that is clearly the "winner." What then?

You may come out ahead at one company on medical but be behind on 401(k). Now you need to match that analysis with what you really need. For example, if you are healthy it might be okay that your prospective employer has, for example, a larger employee premium and a higher deductible. In that case, the medical plan is really an overstatement for you because you are not a heavy user of health-care benefits. But if you are really concerned about your medical benefits because you or your dependents have several medical conditions, then you want to take a close look at that. In addition, it will also be important to confirm that pre-existing conditions will be covered from the moment you start working at the new company—and not after a period of six months, a year, or longer.

There are other considerations too, such as whether your doctors are included in the preferred provider network of the health plan offered by the new company. If you or one of your dependents have been seeing a particular physician for some time and that doctor isn't in the network of the new company's insurance plan, you will either have to change doctors or pay more out-of-network expenses.

• • •

How much information about a prospective new employer's benefit plan is available? Can you just ask the benefits department of the new company for the information?

Sometimes it's difficult to get that information. At times it may feel like you're in the puzzle palace. They won't always tell you. Or they'll hand you a huge binder of information to wade through. There are alternatives. Some companies have Web sites that spell out their benefit plans. In addition, when it comes to large companies in particular, there are alternative Web sites that may be run by employees or former employees that give information about the firm.

The best approach, however, is to do your homework. This means starting early, before you enter the job search or as soon as a headhunter calls you.

NEGOTIATING FOR RELOCATION EXPENSES

THE TRAP: You accept the relocation package that the company offers without question.

THE LESSON: You've accepted an offer to work for a company in another part of the country. Your new employer has offered a flat amount to cover relocation costs, and you don't bother to ask if there is any flexibility in that offer. You take the job and have to dip into savings to cover the rest of the moving costs. You start your new job on a sour note that colors your perception from day one.

THE TIP: Relocation packages are often negotiable. Do a realistic financial analysis of the cost of the move, and make your request accordingly.

What are some of the other things that human resources may not readily tell you? In other words, how can people best be prepared with the right questions to ask?

There are a ton of questions—a real laundry list of issues. Some may apply to one person but not to another. For example, some companies classify jobs according to certain grades. Your status in the company goes up when you reach a certain grade. Then you're included with those who automatically get four weeks of vacation and are eligible for other perquisites, for example being sent to a couple of professional conferences every year. There are other considerations too when it comes to your job grade, such as how it affects your pay now and in the future. HR may try to slot you in a lower pay grade in order to save salary dollars, but that might cap the amount of money you'll earn later on unless you're promoted to the next pay grade. This may be something you'll be able to find out through your discussions with HR, or it may be difficult to obtain this information. Either way, you need to be aware of whether your prospective employer groups jobs according to pay grades in order to see how it might impact your salary.

• • •

Sometimes this information "leaks out" as part of job offer negotiations. I know of a person who works for one bank and who was recruited to go to work for another one. In the course of negotiating the job offer, which involved a very slight salary raise, the HR person told him that he was at the top of the pay grade for nonmanagers at that company.

This is very good information and is worth paying close attention to. What this indicates is there is a boundary or a dotted line between what nonmanagers and managers receive at this company. Going into this job, he has to know that he's at the top of the nonmanager grade, which could limit his pay in the future and even the benefits he receives unless he becomes a manager.

• • •

What about other health-related benefits, like wellness, on-site fitness centers, and other programs that companies offer? Is this a consideration?

Companies that offer wellness programs—cholesterol screenings, smoking cessation clinics, disease management classes, and so forth—are saying something about their cultures. These companies, which are typically larger firms, are putting an emphasis on the value of employee health.

There are other considerations, however. Some companies may offer incentives, such as reduced health-insurance premiums, for employees who participate in a wellness program, who make progress in areas such as weight loss and fitness, or who stop smoking. They can charge more for those who are "unhealthy." Depending upon your health, you should know whether you are likely to benefit from such an approach or not. While the wellness approach sounds like a good idea, if you're overweight, you smoke, and you have diabetes, unless you're going to change your health and lifestyle habits, you may be better off with a company that is less "enlightened."

• • •

What about educational and training benefits? How important are these to the prospective employee, and are they negotiable?

Opportunities for training and further education—including full or partial tuition reimbursement—may be more important to some people than others. In all cases, it is indicative of an employer that values the growth and development of its employees. Large companies will tend to have formal policies regarding training and educational benefits, but even here there is room for negotiation. If you are involved in external training or education or want to do so in the future, then by all means ask for this to be covered in your negotiation process. Be prepared to build a case for the benefit the organization will receive from you taking the training. The stronger the case, the more likely they will pay for it.

Smaller companies may not have any formal policy for education or training. Here again, making the case for the value of the training to the company will help your negotiation. This is another area where a signing bonus might cover the loss of the benefit from your last employer.

• • •

What about pensions? Certainly they are not as prevalent as they were in years past, although they can still be found in certain professions and industries. For example, teachers and state or civil-service employees have pensions. Pensions are also fairly common in certain smokestack industries. If you are in line to receive a company pension and you are thinking of changing jobs, what are some of the issues that you must take into consideration?

Fewer and fewer companies are offering pensions to newly hired employees in favor of a 401(k) or similar plan. However, if you're coming from a company that has a pension and you're thinking of going to another employer, you must think carefully about what you'll be giving up.

Pension plans typically have steep curves that accelerate the value of a pension the longer someone works at the company and the more money a person makes. If you leave the company, you may be right at that threshold where you were about to realize these two big drivers of a value of a pension: length of service and salary. If your pension is based on a percentage of your final pay, you're missing out on a lot if you leave before those final years of service. The third driver is vesting, which is when you'd be eligible to draw your pension.

• • •

At what age would someone be eligible for pension vesting? Is it age fifty or older?

There is a hidden subsidy in a lot of pension plans—that is, it's hidden to all but a handful of people who know what they're looking for. Here's how it might work: When an employee reaches the age of fifty or fifty-five, they receive a huge subsidy to their pension plan. That subsidy can be worth twice a year's pay. We refer to it as "the cliff."

Let's look at a real-world example. You've been accruing pension benefits that will commence at age sixty-five. As you work for the company over the years—at age forty, forty-five, forty-eight—you are earning more pay and more pension benefits. Then you hit the early retirement eligibility age of, say, fifty. Up until that point, the benefits would have commenced at age sixty-five. Now that benefit is available to you at an early retirement age. It's like you've just tacked on an extra fifteen years of service! Now that value is in your pocket. At age fifty, you could leave the company and get a lump-sum retirement. It's even possible that you could go back to work at the same company—or another one—the next day and earn additional salary on top of your pension.

• • •

So the big issue here for someone who is leaving a company that offers a pension is how much is she missing out on by leaving?

For middle-aged employees who are in a defined-benefit pension plan, it's a real consideration. They need to understand where they are on that pension curve. They could be taking a big hit in lost pension benefits.

Another consideration is retiree medical benefits. Let's say Company A has retiree medical benefits that could kick in around age fifty-five or later. That's tough to walk away from.

• • •

But if I'm forty years old and I work for a company that offers a pension, and I get a job offer from a company that has a 401(k) plan but not a pension, how can I calculate what value I'm walking away from?

In reality, it's very difficult. Actuaries can do it for you. (The American Academy of Actuaries, *www.actuary.org,* offers a Pension Assistance List (PAL) program, for people who have questions about their pension.) Some people who are naturally good at complex calculations—for example, engineers—might feel more comfortable setting up a spreadsheet to figure this out, but otherwise it will be hard to estimate.

However, the *fact* that you have a pension with your current employer and your prospective employer offers a 401(k) plan should give you some leverage when you negotiate your job offer. This may very well help you to get a more lucrative job offer, whether in salary, signing bonus, accelerated vesting, and/or other benefits.

• • •

Once again, it comes down to doing your homework.

If you do the research, you will create the opportunity to make the case for yourself based on what you are leaving behind—and what you want your new employer to do for you. If you are a hot property because you have valuable experience in a competitive market, the company may be willing to "pay up" for you. The goal will be to "make you whole" on what you're going to be losing by leaving your current employer.

• • •

At what point in the job offer discussion does all this come into play? Do you address benefits concurrent with salary? Is it a separate issue? Is it something you bring up at the end?

The most important thing to remember is to make sure that you do address it. Too often, in the excitement of getting a job offer, people gloss over the benefits portion. They're handed a package explaining the benefit plan, but they're so focused on other things—such as salary, job title, advancement opportunities, and so forth—that they don't pay much attention to the benefits. As you are presented more and more details about the job offer, including the benefits that the company offers, you want to be prepared with the questions to ask.

• • •

And keep in mind that what looks like a non-negotiable may, in fact, be open for discussion—if an employee is being recruited and can make a good case.

In general, HR will portray solid walls around things that they choose to adopt as practice. Some of those things, however, are practices that can be altered—and all legally and within the realm of the overall recruitment process.

• • •

But will the HR person automatically give you more than what the company is offering just because you ask or you make a good case?

For most HR people, one of their top priorities is to make sure that everybody receives the same things. That's their goal. HR people hate exceptions, so they make it their job to put everyone in the same box. To be fair to the HR folks, the bigger the company, the fewer exceptions that they want to make. The HR department usually has drawers full of one-off deals that were exceptions that had to be made for this one or that one. Then new management comes in and says, "This will never happen again in benefits!" Even if that's the case and benefits can't be changed, there is still the opportunity to make up for what is lost through a signing bonus.

The operating person who is hiring you, however, wants to get you on board. This person is more likely to stretch things for you. In your conversations with the operating manager or hiring manager who wants to bring you into the company, you will have a better chance of selling the need to be made whole in terms of benefits. Then let the operating manager deal with HR.

The concept of being made whole in employee benefits is a growing concept. All you're asking for is to be treated fairly. If you don't pay attention to the benefits being offered to you, then—in terms of vacation, retirement plan vesting, and so forth—you could end up back at square one.

•   •   •

And with the bias in job offers toward salary, you could end up with a loss in benefits and not even be aware of it.

That's why if I were serious about changing jobs, in order to do the best I could in negotiation, I would do a dry-run comparison. I would do an inventory of my current benefits. And then I'd call my friend or neighbor and explain that I want to practice comparing benefits. Without getting into salary, I would ask if I could take a look at that person's benefits and see how we stack up.

This is a very valuable exercise. For one thing, you'll quickly realize just how tough this is. At the same time, you'll also prioritize what is important to you and what is not. It's better to collect this information and have the analysis in hand than to go into the job negotiations blind when it comes to benefits.

Understanding Your Benefits Package

Taking a new job may result in some differences in the benefits that you receive. For example, you may have four weeks of vacation at your current job, but the new position only offers two the first year and three after five years. Your medical insurance premium may be lower at the new job, but the deductibles for in-network and out-of-network expenses are higher.

As a skillful negotiator you need to know what you're currently receiving in terms of benefits in order to pursue a strategy of being "made whole." For example, higher medical costs that you'll face in the future could be offset by a signing bonus. Or, you may be able to negotiate for more vacation sooner in order to continue the level of vacation time that you now enjoy. You won't be able to ask, however, unless you have carefully studied the benefits you currently receive.

If you are employed, fill out the following table of benefits in your current job. Find out whom you need to talk to in order to gather that information, and follow through to gather it as comprehensively as you can. Make sure that you understand as many aspects of your benefits package as possible.

Your Current Position

Vacation _____

Medical premium I must pay _____

In-network deductible _____

Out-of-network deductible _____

Dental premium I must pay _____

401(k) company contribution _____

Current 401(k) vesting _____

CHAPTER SEVEN

Valuing the Feminine Style:
Negotiation for Women

with Judith Wright

Mary is a division president for her company. As a manager, she nurtures her employees, who feel affirmed and appreciated. Common themes expressed by employees in her division are that it's a fun place to work, people love what they do, they are willing to take risks and stretch themselves because they feel supported, and they are loyal to Mary and would do anything to help her. People in her division get projects done with excellence: working extra hours, delivering quality results, and treating their customers the way they are treated—with respect and appreciation.

Kathy was highly qualified for a marketing executive position and made it to the final interview round. In the end, however, she wasn't offered the job. Later, when she had an opportunity to ask why she didn't get the position, she was told she didn't seem "tough" enough. When Kathy asked for an example of what had given that impression, she was told that when she was asked about her weaknesses, she went on for several minutes about all her weak points—over-explaining and even apologizing. A few weeks later, a colleague told her that the job had gone to a man who was less qualified but was clearly better at responding to questions about his weaknesses.

What Kathy saw in retrospect was that she was using candid self-disclosure as a way to establish relationships. Although women often share confidences as a way of building rapport, Kathy realized in this case that she overused the skill without countering it by also sharing the active steps she is taking to overcome her weaknesses. Nor did she extol her strengths to the same degree.

As the two scenarios demonstrate, in the world of work there is both enormous opportunity and potential risk today for women. The strengths and qualities that women bring to the work force—building rapport, establishing and valuing relationships, and promoting win/win outcomes—are needed. Yet, the work world in general and corporate America in particular is still learning to value these qualities, even as women themselves feel more secure about them.

As women approach the job negotiation process, all other points discussed in this book apply. Women, like men, need to do their homework, research the market for their skills and experience, consider the value that they bring, define what they value, understand corporate culture and the environment that best suits them, evaluate their benefits, and follow all the other advice offered in this book.

Specific to women, this chapter seeks to empower them by recognizing the strengths of feminine qualities and also addressing the challenges that women face if they aren't aware of their unique approach and traits. Further, we will purposefully go counter to the advice that many women have heard for decades and to their detriment. Advice such as "negotiate like a man" and "learn to play the game the way they do" only serves to denigrate the feminine. Instead, as women embrace the strengths that they bring and showcase their qualities in the best possible light, they will obtain the outcomes they desire in negotiation. Moreover, the workplace (and the world in general) will benefit from greater balance of the masculine and the feminine.

Judith Wright—educator, world-class coach, lifestyles expert, inspirational speaker, bestselling author, and corporate consultant—is an expert in masculine and feminine communication and committed to increasing the world's value of the feminine in the workplace. She first rose to national prominence in academia, where she designed cutting-edge programs to help adults with disabilities attend college and developed nationally recognized model programs to support children with disabilities and their families. She has since been revolutionizing the personal growth industry, founding SOFIA (Society of Femininity in Action), an organization that promotes feminine values and power, and cofounding the Wright Leadership Institute in Chicago with her husband, Bob, to help individuals, couples, families, and corporations attain more meaning, fulfillment, and success.

A sought-after speaker and expert in areas such as relationships, creative conflict, work productivity, wellness and lifestyle, women's leadership training and development, and more, she has been a keynote speaker for numerous events, conferences, and corporations, including Aetna, A. C. Nielsen, JPMorgan Chase, Kellogg, and the Society of Women Engineers, among many others. She is the author of *The Soft Addiction Solution* (a former edition titled *There Must Be MORE Than This*), and *The One Decision*.

• • •

Can you tell us what your thinking is on the differences between men and women and how that is affecting our workplaces?

There is a body of research that, although conducted and amassed over the last thirty years, is only recently coming to light. Now with the advent of MRIs, CAT scans, and other technology, the research shows undeniably that there are very real neurological and biological differences between men and women as well as related psychological and sociological differences. The fact is, the brains of men and women are constructed differently, and they process information differently. As a result, men and women in the same situations may have very different perceptions, reactions, and behaviors. Men and women facing the same situation, event, or stimulus will process it differently. Consequently, these differences manifest in unique masculine and feminine traits, skills, behaviors, and communication styles that certainly have impact on our workplace interactions. Of course, most men and women exhibit varying aspects of these masculine and feminine traits; for example, men can be nurturing and women can be direct and aggressive. While I refer to these attributes and values as feminine or masculine, they can exist in both men and women.

Traditionally, feminine attributes and strengths have not been acknowledged or valued in the workplace, which has resulted in women not being fairly compensated for contributing their unique gifts and abilities. We have been missing out on the full possibilities of the powerful, synergistic combination of masculine and feminine traits in our businesses.

• • •

Why do we need to address these differences between men and women at all?

As women, we have fought hard over the last decades to establish equality between the sexes. We've made many inroads and victories in a wide variety of arenas. And yet even at our most successful, the picture is incomplete. In our fight for equality, we have tended to assert that women are the same as men, which as the research shows is simply not true. In fact, we have overlooked our most potent advantage and gift—that we are different from men. Our differences carry a more important and even more profound message. As women, we are not meant to be men. In fact, the world, including its corporate manifestations, needs our unique perspective, traits, approach, and vision. This does not mean that we discard our masculine traits. In fact, we critically need those traits to fulfill our mission. But instead of focusing on becoming men, we must instead turn our focus to leveraging our masculine skills in service of our feminine qualities. This is the greatest gift we have to offer.

But as a corporate working woman, how does one negotiate this unfamiliar territory? In a world that has been driven by masculine values, how do we make a stand for feminine qualities and still compete, still succeed, still advance? These are the issues we're facing now.

• • •

We are in the second generation of women in the work force. According to the U.S. Department of Labor, women represent 46 percent of the total U.S. labor force and are projected to account for 47 percent of the total labor force in 2014. Women will also account for 51 percent of the increase in total labor force growth from 2004 through 2014. How has this helped promote the value of the feminine in the workplace?

Despite the number of women employed today, much of the working world is still in the early stages of adjusting to the role of the feminine at work. There is still much to be done to recognize and value the strengths of the feminine, including, and sometimes especially, by women.

Understanding and valuing the feminine is also an asset for men who can also seek to build rapport and relationships in their interactions. Moreover, when men are negotiating with women—from one side of the table or the other—understanding the strengths of the feminine and the masculine will lead to more effective and successful communication between them.

As more and more women enter the work force, their positive impact will be increasingly experienced and valued. At the same time, our business culture is also changing, where traditionally masculine attributes such as quantitative ability, analytical skill, and logical, linear, sequential skills are no longer sufficient. Routinized intellectual work—IT, customer service, financial services and so on—is increasingly being outsourced offshore. As a result, our business culture is moving from a logical, linear, knowledge base to an increasing need for empathizers, relational thinkers, and relationship builders—which are feminine attributes.

THE FEMININE STYLE

THE TRAP: You undersell yourself because you don't value your feminine gifts.

THE LESSON: Maria does not sufficiently value her own contribution to her team's success because she has not been the "hot dog star" or the aggressive competitor that some of her counterparts are. Because she does not sufficiently value the ways she holds the team together, how she brings out the best ideas from each of the team members, and the way she encourages everyone to perform at their best, in the interview process she does a poor job of communicating her strengths and the value she brings. As result, the job offer she receives is considerably less than it would have been had she demonstrated her gifts and value contribution.

THE TIP: Appreciate and communicate the value your feminine gifts contribute.

• • •

Can you give some specific examples of these masculine and feminine traits?

Masculine traits include the drive for results, aggression, action-orientation, logic, the ability to focus on one thing, and a hunter mentality. One of the positive aspects of these qualities is getting a job done. More action-oriented, the masculine emphasizes outcome. The masculine has greater separation between emotion and communication and is less attuned to the nonverbal cues (their own and others). The masculine perceives negotiation simply as conflict and a contest to be won.

You can see the contrast between the masculine and the feminine when it comes to conflict and competition on the playground with young children. When boys play together and conflict arises, there is a fight until someone wins or dominates, and then the game resumes. When girls play and there is a conflict, they start over.

The challenge with masculine traits, if they don't have the balance of feminine perspective, can include a lack of sensitivity, the creation of "losers" in the win/lose mentality, and a lack of fulfillment that comes from not recognizing emotions. When the workplace is masculine-dominated, these aspects are often highly valued. This is the reason many women have adopted these characteristics in order to succeed.

Among the feminine qualities, the strengths include rapport, relationship, nurturing, fostering win/win outcomes, multitasking, relational thinking, acknowledging and accepting feelings, and caring about everyone involved. Women also have the ability to take in a lot of data, which means they are constantly picking up and interpreting all kinds of stimuli from their environment. At the same time, women need to be aware that without the balance of masculine traits there can be detrimental outcomes, including being overwhelmed by their multifocusing, becoming overly self-critical, putting the needs of others ahead of their own to their detriment, tending to talk too much at times, such as when they're nervous, and overfocusing on relationships to the exclusion of getting things done.

· · ·

This is fascinating. Tell us more about the masculine brain and the feminine brain.

This has been a highly controversial topic because we confuse "different" with "wrong" or "inferior." More and more researchers and scientists, however, are exploring the differences between the male and female brain, which are observable from birth. For example, research shows that girl babies are more interested in people and faces than boys are. In fact, in the first three months of her life, a baby girl's skill in eye contact and face gazing increases 400 percent, while a little boy's ability remains the same. Girls are more sensitive to sound than boys and are better able to sing on key. No surprise, then, that women are more discerning about verbal cues such as tone of voice and even subtle variations in pitch.

Because of the increased conductivity between the hemispheres of her brain, a woman is better able to multitask. It also explains her intuition, which is the product of synthesizing information from both sides of her brain. A woman's speech centers and emotional centers are connected in her brain, so she is able to put speech to her emotions and communicate her feelings. In a man's brain, his speech centers and emotional centers are separated.

Masculine strengths lie in different areas. For example, they have better hand-eye coordination and are better able to see patterns and abstract relationships. Males have greater spatial ability and tend to be better at things like reading maps. Men's brains are more compartmentalized, so that they are able to focus on one task at a time. Men have larger brain centers for action and aggression.

•　　•　　•

How would some of the differences between men and women be manifested in a situation such as negotiation?

For one thing, women are more verbal. In terms of words and word units (which include words, gestures, and utterances), a man uses about 7,000 a day on average. A woman uses 20,000. Also women, on average, talk twice as fast as men. So overall, a woman will speak more when negotiating than a man will and will speak more quickly.

Since the emotional center of a woman's brain and the speech center of her brain are connected, she has greater access to her feelings and can put words to them—more so than a man, whose emotional and speech centers of the brain are not connected. So during negotiation a woman is more likely to be aware of her feelings, which can affect her negotiation.

Also, a woman is scanning her environment all the time and is far more aware of and dependent on visual cues, whereas a man has a narrower focus. So on the one hand, a woman is better able to read what's going on with someone based on that person's facial expression, body language, and tone of voice. If a woman can leverage and stay aware of this gift, she may be able to make minor adjustments in her negotiation to a positive outcome.

•　　•　　•

What are some of the potential pitfalls for women resulting from the differences in communication styles?

Because of a woman's brain configuration and the way her mind works, her communication pattern will tend to be more circular. Being more focused on relationships and rapport, women tend to share more of their process rather than deliver a result or bottom-line conclusion. However, in a business setting, if a woman talks more circularly, there is a danger that a man will look at her as not intelligent, organized, or able to get to the point. A woman needs to be aware of this communication style and how men may perceive her.

Also, different communication techniques have different meaning for men and women. For example, for women, interrupting is a sign of agreement; it signifies, "I understand and am following where our conversation is going." For men interrupting is a sign of a challenge or hostility. So while a woman may interrupt during a negotiation to express agreement, a man may be reading that as disagreement.

Understand that both styles are valuable. The feminine style is geared more toward building a rapport and creating a bond with another person. It establishes a sense of mutuality. The masculine style of communication gets the job done. It identifies action and moves on it.

We need both the masculine and the feminine to work synergistically. Both are valuable, and they complement each other: task and relationship, conflict and resolution.

• • •

Let's look at the contrast between the masculine and the feminine approach to negotiation. How would you describe the different approaches?

Negotiation implies that there is some sort of conflict, because one person wants something that is at least a little bit different from what the other person wants. There is an inherent tension present. The masculine style is more competitive with a win/lose approach. The basis of the masculine approach is that there is only so much to go around, so "I better get mine." It is based in scarcity, and therefore someone has to win and someone has to lose.

The feminine approach is to seek to find a solution that allows both parties to win. The strength of the feminine approach to negotiation is to pursue a creative solution in order for everyone to be satisfied. In fact, it's often a solution that would not have been discovered if they had not been seeking a win/win.

On the downside, however, because the feminine is so invested in rapport and building relationships, a woman may accommodate everyone else's needs and not take care of her own. This may be evidenced in the use of compromise to reduce tension in an attempt to preserve a relationship that is not to her full benefit. This can be a decent accommodating strategy, but it is less effective than the result of a synergistic win/win.

•   •   •

What I hear you saying is that through the feminine approach a woman can use her skill of seeing all perspectives to negotiate more creatively based on what she has to offer and work toward what is acceptable as a "win" for both parties.

That's the point. A woman can acknowledge the validity of the point on the other side of the table while still holding her own position. She can find creative ways to honor the other's point of view while at the same time honoring her own.

It's also a feminine attribute for a woman to look at the needs of everyone, but at the same time she should be looking specifically at her own needs and wants. She should make demands at the time when the company is making her an offer. She needs to ask herself how she can leverage this unique opportunity. If she has a big family reunion in six months and she is going to need time off then, this is the time she needs to bring that up. Or if she takes a class on Tuesdays, this is the time to make that schedule arrangement. When the company is making an offer it is usually the time when management is willing to bend the most. A woman should present her needs and wants, though not in a way that makes her look like she's high maintenance; rather, she should do it in a way that demonstrates she is worthy of respect and accommodation.

WHEN THEY WIN AND YOU DON'T

THE TRAP: You compromise in your negotiation so that the company wins, but you feel as if you have lost.

THE TIP: Eva was a middle manager whose husband was a university professor, and she moved with him across the country when he landed a new position with a prestigious university. After a few months of looking for work, Eva found a company that she was excited about. The firm offered her a position at compensation below what she was looking for. Fearing that she would not get the position, she accepted it, even though she felt that the company won while she had lost. Eva never got over that feeling, and her job performance suffered because she felt she was unfairly treated and that the company did not deserve her maximum contribution.

THE TIP: Go for win/win. If you're not satisfied, don't do it.

Given the feminine style of communication and the feminine approach to negotiation that you just covered, what do you see as some of the challenges women might perceive or face in job offer and salary negotiation?

The challenge and opportunity for women is to turn their feminine inclination toward establishing rapport and relationships into a negotiation strength. Rather than shying away from taking a stand or advocating for themselves based on their skills and accomplishments, women can view every negotiation as an opportunity to build and enhance self-esteem and self-worth.

Negotiating from the feminine perspective is completely different from the advice that is widely promoted and evidenced in the workplace, which is to "negotiate like men." In fact, this traditional advice dishonors women and robs the workplace of the feminine values of rapport and relationships that are so needed in business, community, government, and other places of leadership.

With greater understanding of the differences in feminine and masculine approaches, women learn how to be highly effective in negotiating. They will feel empowered to take a stand for themselves and value their own needs and perspectives as much as other people's.

In honoring the feminine, women act with greater authenticity and leadership—and display those qualities in negotiation. Feminine power in negotiating allows for self-confidence and self-doubt to coexist. As women appreciate their own value, skills, knowledge, and expertise, they gather around them others with complementary skill sets and experiences. They use their strengths in rapport and relationships to create highly effective and high-functioning teams.

A woman who values her unique feminine strengths is aware of how much they have contributed to her success, and she is able to articulate these in an interview. A woman who can demonstrate her value through her own performance and by inspiring and mentoring others will shine in the negotiation process.

• • •

How can a woman use the feminine value of achieving win/win in salary negotiation?

I think it's important for everyone, but especially for women, to see that it's not just about salary. The issue is not just how much money she will make—although money is important because of what it represents in terms of value and respect. A woman wants to get a raise from her last job and to be on par with others. At the same time, it is possible to look at salary and the whole job offer package from a win/win perspective.

For example, maybe the company really does have a salary cap; maybe there is only so much that they can do with salary. The woman has to ask herself: What do I really want? Maybe she is willing to take a lower base salary because she negotiates for a larger upside with bonuses based on performance. Maybe there are other valuable aspects of the job, such as a great opportunity to learn new skills, participate in a unique in-house training program, to work with an experienced or revered mentor, or to go back to school through tuition benefits. Maybe she can negotiate to work for different people or even divisions within the company to enhance her skill base and her job satisfaction. Maybe she negotiates for more flexibility in hours, educational benefits, or time, or mentoring, or professional affiliations. All of this can be brought together in a bigger package of what would make the company happy and what would make her happy if she opens up to feminine strengths of relationship and win/win through creative solutions. There is a bigger picture that helps her win beyond the dollar value.

•　　•　　•

Let's take a look at some specific examples of women in negotiating situations—particularly those in which a woman has not felt she has presented herself well or been in full command of her feminine strengths. One woman, Patty, told me a story of being in an interview with a man who did not give much verbal or nonverbal feedback. There were silences after she would finish speaking or answering a question that were uncomfortable for her—so much so that she would try to fill up those silences

with more talking. When she did not get the job, she said she felt she talked too much and "in circles."

If Patty had that discussion with another woman it would have been a much different interaction. Women give each other cues when they speak such as with eye contact, nodding, agreeing, or responding. If Patty had engaged in a circular conversation with a woman hiring manager, she might have had a different outcome. They both might have felt in rapport and the hiring manager might have been positively predisposed to hire her.

In the situation with the man, however, Patty was trying to get cues from him, either verbal or nonverbal. She needed to know that he had understood her, but she didn't know how to read the silent spaces in between. She was looking for visual cues that she's okay, because like most women she was trying to please the other person. So what happened? Chances are she misinterpreted his silence as disapproval. She was nervous and so she talked more, which is what many women do. And when she didn't get the response or acknowledgement that she was hoping for, she tried saying something else in hopes of getting a response.

• • •

Let's say that Patty realizes that she's nervous and is talking to fill up the spaces and is aware of the potential danger of talking in circles or saying too much. What could she do in the midst of the interview to stay in her feminine strengths of building rapport and establishing a relationship with the interviewer, without going to an extreme and sabotaging his impression of her?

One thing that she could do is ask for feedback. For example, she could say, "I've given you a lot of information. What do you think of it so far?" Asking for feedback—"what is your impression of that"—

puts her in a position of strength and establishes a relationship by drawing out the other person.

The problem, however, is that in situations such as these—when someone is not responding or giving much, if any, feedback—women try to "mind read" and guess or anticipate what's going on. The fact is, the interviewer could have been thinking about anything—and quite possibly something that has nothing to do with her. Therefore, it's not for her to guess and try to respond to what she imagines he's thinking.

She can also use this as an opportunity to interview the interviewer, to use her relationship skills to find out more about the company and the position and to establish a more mutual give-and-take within the interview. This establishes a more equal power base, and she'll focus on finding out if they are a fit for her, not just trying to be a fit for them. She can establish more mutuality and power by remembering that she is a buyer, not a seller, in this negotiation.

• • •

When the interviewer didn't respond to her, Patty automatically concluded that there was something wrong with her, and she tried to make up for it. As an interviewer, I know that there are times when there is silence because I'm thinking, usually about the person and the job. There will be a few moments of silence, then I'll ask a question. That's not a negative.

She was taking it personally, when it could just be how he communicates. She jumped to the conclusion that "He doesn't like what I'm saying" or "I've lost the job already," which made her more nervous, and she reacted by talking more and saying things that were irrelevant. Women are trained to be people pleasers, and when Patty didn't get any positive cues, she tried many things to elicit a response. Overfocused on his response, she forgot that an interview is a mutual process where both parties need to be pleased if it is going to be a right fit.

• • •

Let's assume that Patty was able to feel more empowered in the interaction even though she was uncomfortable with the silences and the lack of response and feedback. How could she ensure that she was presenting the most relevant information?

One way is to ask. For example, let's say she has been discussing a project that she has been involved with or explaining her contribution to a team. She can ask, "Are you interested in knowing more about that?" The purpose is to find out what information the other person wants without guessing by saying a million things in hopes that one of them is the right one.

• • •

Reflecting on the interview, Patty also recalled that the more nervous she became, the more her body language reflected it. She sat forward, practically at the edge of her seat, with her shoulders hunched.

It's very easy to appear overeager and overinvested, because it's so important for a woman to get the social cues that she is accepted. Without those cues, she will try harder, and it may result in her looking too eager and desperate by putting her in a position in which she appears to be begging. This is a disadvantage to her. By staying conscious and aware, particularly of her own verbal and nonverbal communication, a woman can stay focused on how she wants to be perceived. Remembering that the interviewers should want to please her as much as she wants to please them will help bring back her sense of equanimity.

• • •

Here's another scenario shared by a woman. In the midst of a session with multiple interviewers, all firing questions at her, JoAnn felt overwhelmed. She got rattled and lost track of which question she was answering. She felt her performance was poor, and she did not stand up to the pressure.

There is a skill I teach called a "One Decision." A One Decision is an overarching commitment you make to the quality of your life. One person's One Decision may be "I stand for truth." Another person's decision may be "I live life as an adventure." The specific decision varies for each person. What matters is that people make a bigger commitment and use it as a compass. In JoAnn's situation this might have been a very helpful point of reference for her. As women we take in so much data, we are constantly scanning and processing stimuli and information from our environment. Behind the scenes, we are constantly making thousands of small decisions to adjust to that environment. With a One Decision we have one solid point of orientation that can guide us when facing all of these decisions. For example, if JoAnn's decision had been "I stand for truth" she might have decided to say, "I'm feeling a little flooded here. Let me back up and answer that question that you just asked." It's a great tool for women, and men, to remain centered in an environment that can feel overwhelming.

• • •

I was in a similar situation not so long ago with a CEO who was interviewing me. He was firing questions at me rapidly, which was clearly part of his operating style. From my masculine perspective, I knew that what I was supposed to do was stand up to him and challenge him.

I think the important thing to remember in this kind of situation is that you are assessing the situation for a fit, just as he is. Just like in JoAnn's situation you can use a One Decision or orienting principle to guide you. If your One Decision is to live life as an adventure, then take some chances: challenge him back, and see what happens. If your One Decision is to tell the truth, then say it straight: "I get the sense you want me to stand up and challenge you on your approach. Is that the case or are rapid-fire questions just your style?" There is no right or wrong approach. What's important, from a woman's perspective, is that you orient to your own values at the same time remaining sensitive to the fact that his approach and skills may be different from your own. Make sure that you ask the questions you need to, risk being yourself fully, and respond truthfully to ascertain if the job and the company are a right fit for you.

•   •   •

As an executive coach to many professionals, including CEOs, how do you see the feminine at work for greater effectiveness today?

One of the women I have been coaching recently became the chief operating officer of her firm. When we started, she had been the chief marketing officer. What I find very interesting is that her more traditional feminine attributes have been huge assets for her company and for her field. Through her emphasis on relationship and rapport, she has developed an amazing team who love to work together and who achieve stellar results. They empower and support each other, and they are proud of the work they do and the company where they work. This is definitely a reflection of the more feminine side.

The feminine is also very creative, and she has been able to use that to transform her business, which is in an older, bureaucratic industry. As she has looked at how to evolve the culture, she has used her feminine creativity and gifts. She values genuineness and encourages her employees to be genuine and has ensured that the company's advertising reflect that value. In fact, that has become a brand for the company.

Her feminine side has been important in establishing and strengthening work relationships, and it has unleashed a lot of creativity and loyalty. She has also tapped into the masculine side of herself, driving to get things done and to have clearer lines of who is doing what, what is expected, and when. She has been empowering the men and the women around her, believing in their potential and doing what she can to help them actualize it. In addition, she has made difficult decisions, using key financial information to make good decisions.

•   •   •

The more this executive embraced her feminine qualities, the more she excelled—and so did her company. Can you share another example?

Another woman who is a manager in a large insurance company was so aware of masculine and feminine communication approaches that she was able to educate her male boss about the differences and strengths of each. Her intention was not to make him wrong and her right. Rather, she demonstrated to him that her qualities of rapport, building relationships, sensitivity to emotions, and awareness of the needs of others as well as her own were all part of her success as a manager. Because of these qualities she has earned the trust of her staff. She's caring, she mentors others, and people around her do better in their jobs. She takes an interest in the people around her and helps them to develop their skills and competencies. That also has increased their loyalty and desire to help her get things done. Her team works harder and is more productive.

Her boss is seeing excellent results, and she has received three substantial raises in a short period of time as a direct result of sharing these gifts and being more productive and adding value to her organization.

●　　●　　●

I was talking recently to a woman who enjoyed a very successful career "in a man's world" in corporate America. Eight years ago, however, she decided that she wanted out. It was very unsatisfying to her. She made good money, but she was not satisfied. In fact, when I asked her to rate it on a scale of one to 10, with 1 being very seldom satisfied and 10 being extremely satisfied, she said it was rarely higher than a 4. She was in a job that paid her well, but it did not contribute to her happiness and her sense of satisfaction.

Clearly, she did not define her success by what she earned; rather, what mattered most to her was how she contributed to others around her, how appreciated she was, the quality of her relationships in the workplace, and the ability to make a difference. These are the elements that would make a woman feel successful. Making a lot of money and getting a lot of stuff done are more masculine. From the feminine side, relationships, being appreciated, and contributing to others are far more important.

●　　●　　●

Women we've talked to have shared that they have mixed experiences with women bosses over the years. Some have been nurturing and interested in the development of everyone around them. Others have been difficult and not interested in mentoring younger women in particular. Can you comment on that?

Women who have made their way in the business world sometimes needed to be more like men in order to be accepted. They have fought very hard to prove themselves—competing against both men and women. Despite the gains that women have made in the workplace, many women—especially those in leadership positions—may feel like they are hanging on by their fingertips. It may be all she can do to hang on to where she is, so she doesn't see herself in a position of helping someone else. Or she might feel that if she helps someone else, a younger woman might then want her job. Others have felt that they made it without help, and it made them what they are, and it should be the same for others. So few women have been well mentored that they often don't know what it means or how to mentor others. Women often don't realize their own value and don't see that they have that much to contribute to another. It could be a million things. Not to make excuses, but it's important to understand that these women may not feel secure in their own places.

The fact is the percentages of women in higher-level jobs have improved, but not by much. Women can start by becoming mentors rather than looking for a mentor. They can also be more direct in asking for mentoring from women they respect.

● ● ●

I've noticed in business today a much broader integration of the masculine and the feminine than we've seen before. The whole competency movement on which I've focused for the past twenty years is based on integrating task-oriented competencies such as results orientation and initiative with traditionally feminine competencies such as relationship-building, rapport, listening, and developing others. We now have recognition throughout much of the business world that to be successful,

you need both. Given that, how can a woman in business today put more emphasis on the feminine in a way that makes her feel empowered and showcases her value?

The first thing is for women to raise their awareness of the differences between feminine and masculine traits and styles in business communications so that they do not misinterpret or jump to incorrect conclusions based on their own perspective. Understanding these differences can also help them to shift styles where appropriate to be better understood and heard.

At the same time, it is a choice that each of us has to make as a woman to honor feminine values despite our environment. There is a lot being written now about approaches that are more needed and beneficial in business which, ironically, are feminine traits. It's not unusual for a male businessperson to talk about the power of win/win situations, a traditionally feminine approach. There are countless books out now on building relationships for business success, again a feminine approach. But the hard truth is that there will be many bumps in the road on the way to honoring the feminine in the workplace.

As women, we cannot wait for the men to honor the feminine. We must choose to honor feminine gifts and strengths even in the face of them being dismissed or put aside. It is really the only way that we are going to make progress in this realm. As we continue to have more success leveraging these gifts, we will hopefully be making culture shifts that can have ripple effects. Lastly, we must not put down the masculine traits but honor and respect their complementary value. As I said earlier, it's not about one being superior or inferior. What we really need in our business world is the masculine strengths in support of the feminine values. This will be real success in business, not just for women, but for everyone.

• • •

Although this chapter is for women in negotiation, what is the lesson that men can take away from what they've read?

I think there are several. First of all, since men are dealing with women more and more—as colleagues, direct reports, bosses, customers, clients, vendors, and so forth—it's advantageous for everyone to understand the inherent differences in the masculine and feminine, particularly as they relate to communication. If men understand that women are relational—they are wired to establish rapport, seek relationships, and explore win/win outcomes—then they will value these qualities more. Men who value the feminine will see its strengths in the workplace to build stronger teams, promote collaboration, foster mentoring, and develop others. Bringing together the masculine strengths of directness and getting things accomplished with the feminine strengths of establishing relationships and helping everyone to win results in an incredibly powerful combination. The more the workplace—and the world—embraces and values the feminine, the better.

CHAPTER EIGHT

The Winning Combination: Performance and Relationship

with Mylle Mangum

Performance and relationship are the winning combination to establish and advance any career.

There are very few positions in which performance is sufficient to maximally succeed without relationship skills. (Maybe if you're a home run hitter in the major leagues your performance alone would be sufficient to succeed without your teammates or your manager liking you.) There are many positions in which being social, likeable, and communicative will enable you to maintain your job, and you may even succeed to a certain extent. However, to maximize your potential and your career success—as well as your career satisfaction—you need the winning combination of both strong performance and strong relationship skills. These skills will also help you become a more strategic and successful negotiator.

When Dave Jensen was in the job search process, he did not use his network of relationships adequately, nor did he present his performance in such a way as to attract the maximum exposure in his new company. Once he began working in the new position, however, he quickly brought together his solid performance and his ability to establish relationships with colleagues and managers who recognized the value of his experience and knowledge. Dave's performance and his new relationships at work not only attracted positive attention but also improved his prospects for advancement based on the combination of his contributions and the fact that others liked and valued him.

To address the wining combination of performance and relationship, we turned to a highly successful woman in corporate America. Mylle Mangum has had an extraordinary career. After a first job teaching gifted children, she started with General Electric's transportation division, where she was one of only a few women working in a business whose primary focus at the time was production of locomotives and transit cars. During her tenure there, Mylle helped to deliver one of the first-ever real-time, online factory warehousing and production systems for the company. From there, Mylle went to GE headquarters to become part of its corporate consulting business, then on to GE's Power Distribution Equipment Business. Recruited away from GE, Mylle joined BellSouth to start its international division, and progressed to head Strategic Planning for the telecommunications company. Her next move was to Holiday Inn Worldwide as an executive vice president of Strategic Management, then to the international travel company, Carlson Wagonlit. In 1999, she became CEO of MMS Incentives, Inc., a company that sold marketing and loyalty incentives, which gave her unique experience working with a private equity group.

Today Mylle is owner and CEO of IBT Enterprises, LLC, which provides design, build, and consulting services for financial institutions across the country and is now expanding into specialty retail operations. She also serves on the board of directors of six publicly traded companies and chairs two compensation committees, two governance committees, and an audit committee. In addition, she is a member of the Committee of 200 (*www.c200.com*), an organization of women business leaders that promotes opportunities for women in business.

• • •

Throughout your career, you've been in companies and businesses that were male dominated. How did your ability to build relationships, coupled with your performance, help you in your career?

My advice to anyone, woman or man, is this: First, you perform. You don't count on gender or anything else to give you an advantage. You have to count on performance. Being a woman in the GE Transportation division, I understood it's all about business. It can get a little lonely sometimes, but I really had terrific mentors—people, especially in GE, who wanted to help others who had potential and who could perform. GE is a little bit different than other companies in that it's good at identifying and nurturing high-potential people. I was lucky to work with a man who helped me to really understand the business and the people in the business, which was especially important because it was a heavily unionized environment in which we were implementing system changes.

Although I found that being a woman helped in terms of negotiating skills, I couldn't expect it to be a tea party. It was a difficult business environment without much margin for error. It really toughened me up for the business world. There are no free lunches and no free rides; you have to learn to deal in a tough-minded way on the basis of great performance.

• • •

One of the things that people need to embrace, then, is that, number one, you perform.

Yes—and track it! A lot of people, women especially, are reticent to blow their own horns too much. However, performance must be tracked. I always embraced performance measures rather than running away from them. For example, when you're working with technical systems in terms of manufacturing scheduling, you're looking at issues such as how far is the factory behind? What kind of issues are there in terms of costs, timing, and scheduling? Whatever your job goals are, you are going to be measured against those goals. When you are negotiating in terms of salaries and contracts, those are the fact-based discussions you have with your manager.

• • •

These same issues are quite applicable to the interview and job offer process. People want to know specifics about what you did in previous jobs.

They can interview you and find out if you're a nice person, but what you really want to do is provide performance-based, fact-based information that illustrates that you will succeed at the job and the company will benefit from hiring you.

• • •

Clearly you learned what you needed to do—to communicate and be well thought of in a world where doing is much more highly valued than being.

In any situation in which you find yourself—social or professional—you have to learn the "rules of the road" within that culture. It's not about changing the rules of the road. If you think you are going to do that, then remember it is easier to make things better by being on the inside. Hopefully the things that I did helped to pave the way for other women in business, by people finding out that there are women who are performance based. In any situation, you have to discover what is defined as success and then operate within those parameters—or master success from that standpoint.

• • •

How did you find out the "rules of the road?" This is a classic problem for people who are new to an environment—whether women, people of color, immigrants, etc.—and who need to figure out how to be successful.

You listen, and you ask a lot of questions in the beginning. You do your homework and research by talking to a lot of different people, and you find examples of people who are deemed to be successful in that environment. There are a lot of techniques that you can employ until you get your bearings and you are able to understand what's expected of you. One way is to act as if you are a consultant in that business. You ask yourself: What are they trying to achieve here, and how can I help them? I approached every job just like that.

• • •

Getting a mentor at the early stage of one's career or even as a midlevel professional is incredibly valuable. How would you advise someone about how to find a mentor?

I wouldn't start out asking for someone to mentor you. First, you build relationships. For example, in GE, when I started out I knew nothing about programming computers and I was in the middle of an IT division! There was an older gentleman there—he was at a higher level than I was, although I did not report to him—who was assigned to help me learn the technology and the basic elements of programming computers. He and I ended up having a great relationship. People are an amazing source of information if you truly want to learn and expand your horizons. This man was a terrific resource in the business for me, and he helped me understand the value of mentoring.

GOING IT ALONE—AND BEING LEFT BEHIND

THE TRAP: You are the lone wolf and don't ask for help, coaching, or advice.

THE LESSON: Roberta was recently promoted to manager and, in an effort to show what she really could do, never asked for help. Even when colleagues tried to give her coaching or friendly advice, Roberta rebuffed it, saying that everything was going great. As a result, her career stalled. She failed to develop the people skills necessary to succeed as a manager and in a few years found herself back in a technical position at a different company.

THE TIP: Get as much mentoring, feedback, and coaching as you can. You will make a far greater contribution and command more compensation.

I have the benefit of having known you for many years. I appreciate the relationship skills that you have. I remember when I first met you, I could tell you were warm, enthusiastic, and engaging, and you make the people around you feel good. You give attention to people very well. As a consequence of that, people want to help you. People would feel good about themselves for helping you. This goes back to relationship skills that are incredibly valuable. As people give to you, they feel that they are being given to, as well. There is mutuality of giving.

There is a responsibility on the part of the junior person or the one who is learning to make sure that the people who are helping you know that they are helping. I always felt that if someone took time to help me, I had a responsibility to let that person know he helped me. You have a responsibility to succeed, too.

It's a fine web of relationships. The fragile nature of relationships is tricky, especially in business. There are a lot of people, especially when you are succeeding, who won't like it! This can be a real shock. I grew up in a small Southern town; you could stop by anybody's house for lunch. I didn't know there were mean people in the world. When I found them, I was amazed. Therefore, it's very important to have a strong relationship fabric in business so that people know who you are. There are always people who are trying to make your life unpleasant. There are always those who are jealous or who have other agendas. You have to have strength of purpose, personality, and that fabric of relationships to overcome that.

• • •

From the position of being a job candidate, people often feel that they are "sellers" and not "buyers." (See Chapter 10.) It's not uncommon for people to feel as if the organization holds all the cards and they have no power. How does that play out when you are in a situation in which you feel vulnerable and you feel that the decision-making is not yours?

Vulnerability can be magnified depending upon someone's confidence level and experience. It might show more directly in a woman who is less comfortable presenting her accomplishments than it would in a man. Therefore, a woman in this situation might not come across as firm, clear, and confident of what she is worth. She is "selling" and not "buying."

In this day and age, there are a lot of people who are looking for jobs. What companies are looking for, however, is *talented* people, and that's a different story. The issue is to make sure that your talent is appropriately displayed and creates the sense from a corporate viewpoint that you're an asset that this company really needs.

Individuals, I find, many times don't market themselves and package themselves well—and women do that less well than men. My advice is to package yourself and your talents as if you were a service-based business or a group of products.

• • •

How would someone making $100,000 a year as a professional or in a middle-management position do that? Let's say someone has been contacted by another organization, and now that person wants to package herself well. What should this individual do?

I compare it to a product roll out. I always thought about myself in those terms. What are your product qualities? Is it management experience and abilities? Is it efficiency? Creativity? Consistency? With those qualities, what are the deliverables? What have you delivered over the time span of your career, and how is that appropriate to this new environment?

It was very different when I went from GE, which was a business-to-business environment, to BellSouth, and then to Holiday Inn Worldwide, which are all consumer-based. I had to find out what that new environment needed, and then I looked at how my skills fit those needs. I had to identify how to articulate those skills in the interview process with great clarity. I had to ask myself, "How do my skills apply to this environment, and how can I help the company accomplish its objectives?" People have to be extremely deliberate in this process.

• • •

How can you prepare for such a "presentation" as part of the interview process?

One vehicle is to prepare a PowerPoint on your "product." Now, that might turn some people off, but it's a good exercise to help you clearly state what your qualities and deliverables are.

People call me all the time when they are looking for a job or thinking of changing jobs. They'll ask if I can introduce them to someone in a company. Before I ever do that, I ask them to do something: write an introductory letter and treat it as a marketing package. It could be a PowerPoint or it could be black-and-white text in a word document. It forces people to identify what their strengths and skills are, what they have accomplished, and why it would be important for a company to have them as an employee. This works at any level, from entry-level to a senior executive—although senior executives sometimes do a worse job at this than an entry-level person. This exercise helps people to clarify their thinking, and it's a type of thinking that most people don't employ.

• • •

I'd like to address some of your experiences as a woman in the corporate world. What were some of the things you experienced?

This is less true now because there are more women in business, and more women in leadership positions, but when I started out I always found that people were at least curious about what I had to say. I was a bit different because I was a woman. I was a bit of a "special segment." That was a double-edged sword. If a woman performed well, it was highlighted, and if she did not perform well, it was also highlighted.

There were times in my career when I got the interview because I was the only woman in the process. They didn't think I was a candidate, but they had to show that they were interviewing women and minorities. If I could outshine everyone else, it was terrific. I got the opportunity, and then it was up to me to use it.

•   •   •

How did your feminine strengths—rapport and relationships— help you in these situations? You obviously displayed your nurturing qualities, but you also used the more masculine communication technique of directness to make sure you got your share (see Chapter 7).

There is a phrase in the South, where I'm from, "Steel Magnolias," which describes a type of woman. First there is the image of the magnolia, which is a gorgeous, fragrant flower. Every Southern yard has a magnolia. The term Steel Magnolia refers to having a firm inner core of purpose and clarity of direction, coupled with that ability to establish nurturing relationships. It is the best of both worlds.

•   •   •

While establishing a relationship and rapport in the interview process, I'm sure you encountered some problematic interview questions. For example: "Are you planning to have children?" Or there may be more sexist comments. If that happens in the interview process, what is your suggestion?

My advice is to anticipate those things and be prepared with your answers. Let's say someone asks you, "Are you planning to have children?" You can say, "I have no idea how my life will unfold, but all I can say is I will deliver what this business needs." You give your answer without answering the question. Sometimes women get offended or taken aback by these types of questions early on, and don't think to fend them off. My advice is to give an answer, an honest answer, but one that doesn't make a woman look hostile, angry, or upset.

Here's an example, and while I don't remember the specific situation, the question was about me being a woman. I said to the person, "You see, I'm a woman in business and there is not much I can do about that. The best I can see, that has nothing to do with what we're talking about here, which is delivering to the bottom line of the corporation. . . ."

This is good advice for men, too, who may be asked questions that could take them off track, distract them, or make them feel defensive. My advice to anyone is to keep your mind on the goal and keep moving forward, without letting those kinds of extraneous issues get in the way.

A person has to decide if that's the environment in which he or she wants to work. Once you get the job offer, then you can make the decision whether or not to take it.

• • •

When someone in the interview process raises these kinds of questions, a person should ask herself if this is indicative of the corporate culture. Then she needs to consider whether to work in that environment or for that hiring manager who is doing the interviewing.

You are always going to find people in the world—in business or a social situation—who have certain prejudices and biases. Maybe somebody doesn't like red, and you're wearing red. I find people who deal with life and who don't get overly obsessive, who keep their goals in mind, are healthier and better able to deliver. There are lots of women who never make CEO, but there are also lots of men who don't either. Keep your mind on the course and make course corrections as needed.

TRACKING YOUR PERFORMANCE AND SHOWCASING IT

THE TRAP: You hide your talents for fear of "blowing your own horn."

THE LESSON: Laurie understands that her company needs to be satisfied and appreciative of her contribution. She also knows that she needs to use all her gifts fully to contribute the maximum to the organization and to grow and develop herself. She tracks her performance and has no problem showcasing it as an example of the value she contributes to the organization. In interviews, Laurie is not afraid to talk about her ability to establish rapport and make others feel good as she interacts with them in the sales process. At the same time, she demonstrates those skills with the interviewers. With her demonstrated performance and her ability to build relationships, it's no wonder that in her last position Laurie was told that the salary she was offered was the highest the company had ever paid to anyone in a sales position.

THE TIP: To maximum your return, maximize what you give, and make sure that others know.

The overall message, then, is to keep your mind on your goals, build relationships, and keep track of your accomplishments. Package yourself well, communicate that package, and continue to build your substance.

Yes, and back to the idea of substance, it's amazing how many people I meet who haven't proven themselves. They don't feel the need to do so. They have a chip on their shoulder and think that their lack of success is because of somebody else. They don't have a track record of successes related to their own accomplishments and the ability to operate in different environments.

•   •   •

As people manage their careers, both internally with their current companies and externally with new employers, one of the issues they may face is the need for balance between work and personal life. This is particularly a concern for the "sandwich generation" that has school-aged children and older parents. What is your advice for people who are looking to manage their careers well, while achieving work/life balance?

We had a situation in our company involving one of our top interior designers. She needed to have greater flexibility because she wanted to be home at a certain time of day with her pre-kindergarten-aged son. She trusted us enough to ask us about a flexible work arrangement. What's interesting, though, is the arrangement she presented to us involves working longer hours than she did before, but with a flexible arrangement, and she is continuing to do a fabulous job.

The moral of this story is if you are a top performer, you will find there is more flexibility for you. You are not saying that you are a victim of being in the sandwich generation or the victim of having an aging parent. Rather, you want to keep your career goals on track while dealing with other issues. The big issue here is that you are *still* performing.

If performance is going to be an issue because of the situation you're facing, then you need to take a leave of absence. It's better to be upfront and request the leave of absence, saying, "I need this much time off," than to look like you're a nonperformer.

As an aside, people who aren't very happy usually aren't performing at their peak. They are the ones who become complainers and whiners or who have bad attitudes. I will hire a person with a great attitude over a person with great credentials.

• • •

When dealing with work/life balance or the need to deal with family or other issues, how much personal disclosure is appropriate?

What you don't want is to make the company deal with your personal issues. You deal with them and then suggest ways that the company can help you. Sometimes people say, "I've got an aging parent; therefore, I'm not going to be here at times. I'll be coming in late and leaving early." That leaves the company to deal with the issue. A better approach is to ask yourself, "How can I meet my performance criteria—delivering more and better—while still dealing with this issue?" For example, when looking at a shift in work hours, figure out how you can deal with a situation efficiently and not hurt the company. Many people try to force the company to deal with them; successful individuals just deal.

• • •

It goes back to the principle of performance, which is first and foremost. You cannot use relationships to make up for a performance deficit or instead of making the effort to prove that you are a performer. Once you have established that you are a performer, things tend to open up because of the collegial relationships that have been formed.

Once you perform, you will have many more opportunities. Companies are looking for good people who are great performers. People will want to establish relationships with you because of the value you bring. Once you have established a track record, the world will open up to you.

Your Marketing Package

In order to clarify your thinking and gain better focus in your communication as you pursue future job opportunities, develop a "marketing package" for yourself. This may be done in either a PowerPoint presentation or a written document. The objective is to put together a package that highlights key "marketing factors" that would make a company want to "buy" the product—which is you!—and pay you the six-figure salary that you deserve.

Key factors to consider in your marketing package include:

- Your strengths (consistency, creativity, efficiency, etc.)
- Your technical skills (abilities and tasks that you have mastered)
- Strong behavioral competencies (initiative, influence, leadership, communication, teamwork, etc.)
- Accomplishments that you have achieved
- Specific results that your organization has realized at least in part because of your efforts
- Benefits to previous organizations in your work history
- Benefits that you offer to your next employer

CHAPTER NINE

The Employer's Perspective

with William White

The job offer and salary negotiation process is a two-way dialogue between you and your prospective employer. The person on the other side of the table may be your hiring manager, someone from human resources, or another manager. You may meet with several people in the company who will have some say in evaluating you and your fit with the organization. Wouldn't it be helpful to know what is running through their minds during the interview and negotiating process?

One of the assumptions that prospective employees often make is that negotiating a job offer is an adversarial contest, instead of seeing it as the first steps toward establishing trust. For Dave Jensen, negotiation became a contest between him and the company over the salary issue. "I got the impression from HR that they were trying to squeeze me as much as possible to get me to take a lower salary," he recalls.

In Dave's case, his experience may have reflected an HR department that whether by habit or design was not forthcoming about explaining the company's salary structure and the reason he was offered a particular level of pay. As a result, Dave's experience made him feel as if HR "was not as invested in me coming onboard as much as my manager would have been."

If he could do it all over, Dave believes that having more open discussions with his hiring manager in particular would have led to a greater appreciation of value on both sides (see Chapter 2) and a better understanding of pay structure at the company (see Chapter 5). The result would have been more trust—on both sides—from the initial discussion.

Insights into how employers think can help demystify the process for the job candidate and make you feel less as if it's a competition between you and them. Rather, you will see how, from initial interview through job offer and acceptance, you are building what both parties hope is a longterm relationship, one based on mutual respect and attainment of goals that benefit both parties. As William J. White, long-time executive and retired chairman and CEO of a New York Stock Exchange–traded company, advises, it all comes down to your contribution.

Bill spent his corporate career in executive positions at several companies across many different industries, including Hartmarx Corporation, USG Corp., Masonite Corporation, and Mead Corp. He served as chairman/CEO of Bell & Howell Company (now Pro-Quest) from 1990 until 1998, when he retired. After his retirement from corporate life, he became a professor at Northwestern University in the Department of Industrial Engineering & Management Sciences, from 1998 to the present. He was honored as McCormick Teacher of the Year in 2001. A graduate of Northwestern University, Bill received his M.B.A. from Harvard University in 1963. He is also the author of *From Day One: CEO Advice on Launching an Extraordinary Career* (Prentice-Hall, 2005).

• • •

In your long and prestigious career, you've personally hired hundreds of people, and the people whom they've hired have numbered in the thousands. Based on that experience, what insights can you share with us about the process from the employer's perspective?

Let's start at the beginning with why a company needs to hire someone in the first place—namely, to accomplish a certain task, which is composed of a number of activities. The best way to look at this is to use the example of a brand-new start-up. You're the founder, and you've decided that you need to hire another person. That need is usually driven by a set of tasks that can be delegated to that person. As soon as you talk about delegating, you move into two other areas: first, the value of having the tasks done for you and, second, the value system of the person to whom you will delegate the work.

• • •

Therefore right from the beginning, the company's thinking is rooted in the kind of person who would be best suited to accomplish the required tasks. This is aligned with the discussion on corporate culture (see Chapter 3).

Yes, and the reason is simple: In a corporation you must allow for multiple decisions to be made simultaneously throughout the organization. The hope is that these decisions are consistent and aligned. You want members of your team whom you employ to have the same value system as you, the founder. If that person has the same information and data available, chances are that person will make decisions that are consistent with yours—if you had the time to make that decision.

• • •

Once a company has determined that someone needs to be hired and has identified that the person's values need to be aligned with top executives/corporate culture, what comes next from the employer's point of view?

Keeping with the example of the new start-up company, the next step is for the employer to ask, "What is the value of having these tasks done for me?" This step takes a company right to the outside market. In other words, if the company could subcontract for a particular service—maintenance, general purchasing, even using a broker for sales—this would establish a benchmark for the cost of that service. The next step is for the company to think about the benefits of hiring a person, instead, to accomplish those tasks. The sanity test in the process is provided by the marketplace: What are the benefits and costs of hiring someone versus outsourcing the task? Assuming that a company decides to hire someone, the next step would be for the employer to go out and get as much information as possible about what similar people in similar jobs are being paid.

• • •

It's interesting to see the thought process that the employer goes through or has gone through in the past, which then becomes part of the overall recruitment and hiring process. Just like job candidates who go through a process of discovering the market, the jobs they are best suited for, the corporate culture that is a good fit, and so forth, the employer has a similar process for determining its needs and the kinds of people it wants to hire.

As soon as a company begins thinking about hiring someone, the issue becomes the type of person to fit this role. The company determines a set of attributes that it wants for the new hire. This would include the individual's attitude. Is this person looking to see how he/she can contribute to the organization, or is this person only interested in doing well? Certainly you can have both interests, but where is the greatest weight in the person's mind? Where is this person coming from philosophically? Is he or she highly motivated? What goals has he or she set? Does the person see herself as being part of the organization, or is she only looking for a job? Then the employer wants to talk about skills.

•   •   •

Going into the interview process, most people only see that there is a job opening and they want to find out about that job. They want to sell themselves into the job based on their capabilities and experiences. People are not as conscious or aware as they could be as to who it is they are talking to and what the organization is looking for.

It's philosophy first and skills second. The other factor, in addition to attitude, is the personality of the candidate. Is this someone who will fit in comfortably with the work team? Most likely during the interview process, the candidate will meet with more than one person in the organization. The people who are part of the interview process will triangulate on the candidate's personality and all the other factors.

THE VIEW FROM THE OTHER SIDE OF THE TABLE

THE TRAP: Speaking only from your own perspective.

THE LESSON: Throughout the interviewing process, Ignacio continually asked questions and demonstrated interest in the employer's point of view. In addition to asking questions about the company, its competitors, and its problems and opportunities, he was acutely aware that the prospective employer was assessing him. At the end of each interview, Ignacio asked the interviewers what they thought of him in light of their needs. Not only did this give him valuable information and insight for future interviews, it also demonstrated his awareness and listening skills to the company. In addition, it encouraged the interviewers to pull together their thoughts regarding him in a way that helped move his interview process forward toward a successful salary negotiation.

THE TIP: Understand the employer's perspective.

Now let's assume that I'm a candidate and you've been interviewing me for a job. I have the right attitude; my values are consistent with yours. I have a healthy mix of self-interest and the desire to contribute. I have enthusiasm and motivation, and I have the skill set. Now let's say that there is another candidate who fits just as well as I do. As the employer, you have found two candidates who are a good fit. What role does how much each person is currently making play in the final selection?

Generally speaking, this would be the last factor. Two-thirds of the process is to communicate the expectations to the candidate. The reason I went through the discussion earlier about the value of the job is to show that there is a process that drives salary ranges that most organizations have for a job (see Chapter 4). Salary ranges are not arbitrary. When it gets down to compensation, the process becomes mechanical.

If one person who is coming in is being paid more and the other person is being paid less, it won't affect the offer too much—a little bit, but it's not the most important factor. It is a consideration, but not a huge one.

• • •

Based on the salary range and midpoint for the job, how does a company evaluate what it would have to offer each of these two well-qualified and otherwise equal candidates should it decide to proceed with one or the other?

Let's say that one candidate is at the twenty-fifth percentile of the salary range for the job and the other is at the fiftieth percentile. In each instance, the employer is going to think about the attractiveness of the job offer to entice a candidate to come and work for the company. It may be that the offer will be 10 percent, 15 percent, or 20 percent more—based on the total package—for the person who is making less, while the person who is at the higher pay level is seeing a smaller percentage increase in the offer. However, all that depends upon competitive market factors and how difficult it will be to recruit that person.

• • •

When a company looks at what it will take to hire a person away from another position, what are some of the factors that are involved?

Part of it is the enthusiasm that the person has for making a change, which is a subtle thing over and above the person's ability to do the job. Is this person truly enthusiastic about a new opportunity or just "shopping?" From the company's point of view, the amount offered over the old salary to attract a candidate is very much determined by that individual's enthusiasm and the team's evaluation of that person's ability to hit the ground running and make a contribution right away. The more pluses that a person gets in the internal evaluation by the team at the prospective employer, the more the company will be apt to reach for that candidate in terms of compensation. The determining factor is how much the company wants this person, which is a direct reflection of how much that individual is expected to contribute in the long term.

•   •   •

You've been involved in hundreds of hires. Can you give some examples of behaviors or attitudes that turned you off, that made you question the person's suitability for the job and the corporate culture?

One thing would be if the person raised the issue of compensation too early. If that's one of the first questions asked, it shows that this is the most important thing to that person. Now, I must say that much of my corporate background was working in manufacturing operations. Perhaps in an investment bank the motivation would be weighed differently. But certainly from my personal experience—and in companies with similar jobs and it has been fairly well documented—a person will turn off a potential employer if he talks about money first.

A second negative would be a person who says that she is excited about an opportunity but appears to have very little knowledge about what's going on with the company. The person doesn't even have a clear idea about what the company does, either because she hasn't been doing any reading about the organization or she has poor or bad data. Or in some rare cases, the benefits package may be unusually attractive. One company that comes to mind is SAP, a business software company headquartered in Germany, which offers a benefits and perquisite package that is so strong people are sometimes attracted to the company for the wrong reasons.

• • •

Let's say that a person has gone through a first and maybe a second interview, and now the issue of compensation has come up. What are some of the issues that could sabotage how a person is viewed by an employer?

One thing that happens, particularly with young professionals, is an inflated sense of what they should be paid. They have not done a study of what comparable salaries are for a specific job in a particular market. Rather, they have an idea in their heads that is not based on any real data. The person's ideas about compensation probably came from talking to friends. I warn my college students about this all the time: A friend gets a new job and may inflate what he or she is being paid. What happens, then, is that they hear somebody brag about making "X" and they think they should make that too. When a company offers something that is realistic and fair, but less than the number the applicant has in mind, the person thinks he or she is being cheated. Or, someone—particularly a young person—may have established a style of living that forces him to ask for compensation that is driven by the expenses rather than his value to the company. Telling an employer that you must have "X" to live on will sabotage the company's view of you.

Here's another example, and this was a more experienced person who was making a six-figure salary. He believed he needed to have a high-level salary—more than the job was offering. In order to prove that he was willing to take a "risk"—at least as he saw it—he told his employer that he'd be willing to resign after eighteen months if the company took a chance on him and he failed. He thought that by offering to resign he was taking all the risk! What he didn't take into account was what would happen if he came in and did a poor job and was overpaid for his contribution during those eighteen months. Not only would the company not receive a fair value for what he was paid, but other people on his team and in the corporation would be set back because of his poor, unsatisfactory performance. In some cases, particularly with a higher level person, it could take years to recover.

•   •   •

From the company's perspective, what is the danger of an employee who continually brings up salary increases and the need for a raise or promotion?

To look at that situation from the employer's point of view, let me give you another example. In one company I worked for, a man who reported to me was continually demanding higher compensation because he felt that he had done such a good job. He felt it was extremely important that he have a higher salary because he deserved it. What he disregarded, however, was his influence on the rest of his team. He had a social relationship with the CEO of the company, so he thought he was untouchable. He didn't think he had to worry about anybody else on the team or in the department. He kept demanding a higher salary, but I felt he had not earned a raise based on his contribution, especially as a leader of his team.

It got to the point that I told him, "If you continue with this attitude I will have to ask you to leave." He told me, "I have friends in high places." He was surprised when I told him that I had already talked to his "friends in high places," and they agreed: He had to change his attitude or leave.

The bottom line is people often have wrong information about what they "should" be paid based on the marketplace. Second, they have a skewed point of view regarding what their value is to the organization.

Two points come to mind here: One is that employees may not be listening to the feedback that they're getting in their regular appraisals. The second is that they are measuring themselves against their own benchmarks—rather than their boss's expectations for the job. This could be compounded by the fact that many bosses aren't particularly good about giving feedback. In these situations, employees must discern the true message within the information that's being communicated and also be more self-critical as opposed to self-aggrandizing.

Your salary negotiation should be based on your "trading base" with the company. As I explain to my students, when they are starting out, from the company's standpoint, they have nothing to trade except their goodwill and motivation. As people become more experienced, the basis of that negotiation is what can you, the prospective employee, give—attitude, experience, a willingness to contribute—in order to receive more from the company.

• • •

One of the themes that runs through the chapters in this book is the importance of doing one's homework—everything from analyzing current pay and benefits to knowing what the competitive market is for one's skills and experience. Too often people get so hung up in what they think they need and their own economic scarcity that they don't focus on the reality of the marketplace and what's fair.

They are focused on themselves and they may also have bad data about the marketplace. You need to be operating with good, accurate data. There are companies that publish salary data—sometimes it's average salary and other times salary ranges. Most companies, when asked in the interview process, will tell you about the salary range for a job.

There is one twist when it comes to salary data, however. If you were to open the books at virtually any employer and look at the salaries, you would find much inequity. In some cases, a job is misevaluated; in another, a person is overpaid for some historical reason. Or someone is underpaid. The most interesting thing about the argument against publishing salaries is not to hide inequities; rather, it is to keep bosses from having to defend the salaries paid. If supervisors know that every salary that they determine on their own and with their manager's approval will be made public, that puts tremendous pressure on them. It takes a confident manager to do that.

• • •

Speaking of salary and hiring approvals, how does that work in most companies?

Every good system has two levels of approval for hiring and salary changes: the manager involved and also that manager's boss. In the case of the CEO, that secondary approval would be the board of directors.

• • •

From the company's perspective, I would imagine, there is real concern about someone who appears to be "money hungry." Pushing too hard for too much pay will raise the question in the employer's mind about what this person can really deliver.

The person isn't operating with the assumption that if he or she delivers, the reward will come.

There is also the concern that if this person is strictly focused on making more money, then he or she is looking around on the outside for the next opportunity and isn't 100 percent focused on the business at hand. From the corporate perspective, the employer is afraid that this employee is not only pushing the organization but also looking around for the next best deal. Once an employee is marked this way, as "money hungry," it takes a long period of changed behavior to erase that mark.

• • •

Many people come at negotiation from an adversarial position. They say to themselves, "The company wants to get me for as little as they can." Is that accurate? How do employers view the negotiation process?

The important word to think about here is trust. If there is going to be a long-term relationship between a company and its people, there has to be trust. The better the trust, the more successful the relationship. From the company's perspective, there is a responsibility to shareholders not to overpay for people who are hired to do specific jobs. At the same time, the company wants to have a long-term relationship with its employees. The employer wants to develop trust with that person so that six weeks after someone has been hired, he or she isn't out the door.

Most companies approach this process with a desire to be fair and provide people with the opportunity to grow. They don't want to pay them too much, but they want to be fair in compensation. For the midlevel manager, there must be even more trust with the company, because that manager is going to have more responsibility and lead and develop others. If that element of trust is not there, it's not going to be a long-term relationship.

If the job candidate coming into the negotiation process doesn't trust the company, is skittish in every encounter, or is forever asking for more money, that will undermine the relationship. If employees contribute, they will be paid. Employees who are contributors by meeting and exceeding the objectives set for their jobs, the employer will notice. Believe it or not, employers are always looking for that rare person who always exceeds objectives.

If you fit that category you will be noticed and valued. The company doesn't want to lose you. Your boss, someone from HR, or even your boss's boss will make sure that you are continually treated fairly. If you are a super performer, then you will be treated "fair-plus." It's too expensive for the company to recruit someone else. They'd rather keep you if you're a good performer.

•   •   •

There are a number of issues underlying what you're saying here. One is the basic trust issue. There is also a broader market issue that job candidates must understand because of the cost to the company of recruiting, hiring, and training people. The company wants to treat good performers well.

It's not just rational, but also a real economic pressure on the corporation. The company knows that if you don't feel fairly rewarded it will increase the probability that you will change jobs.

•   •   •

What happens, though, if after a year or so on the job—making a contribution, meeting or exceeding expectations, and putting the major focus on the team—a person sincerely doesn't

feel as if he or she is being fairly compensated. What happens then?

If a year or two after being hired a person thinks that there are people who are being treated better, or people who are being paid more for similar work—perhaps in a different department—then it's time to go to the boss or someone else who is influential for a straightforward conversation. The employee needs to look the boss or other person right in the eye and say, "You know I love working here, but I just have a sense that I'm not being treated fairly in terms of compensation. Can you assure me that I am being paid fairly for the job that I'm doing here?"

Now it's down to psychology, and it's amazing what will happen. If the other person—the boss, the person from HR, or someone else—looks the employee in the eye and says, "I'll check on that for you," then the employee can be pretty much assured of being treated fairly. If the person won't look the employee in the eye and says something like, "I'll get back to you," that tells you something as well. Another red flag answer is if the person says, "I can't talk to you about that; it's confidential." Your suspicions are correct at that point, and now you must discern whether the obstacle is your boss or the company's values. If it's your boss, you will have to find an alternate contact in HR, or your boss's boss, which as we've pointed out is very tricky. If it's the company, it's time to seek opportunity elsewhere, because this will not be your last experience of this type if you stay where you are.

The employee's position, however, must be grounded in the right philosophy and attitude. The employee wants to be treated fairly, and if things are not fair, they must be adjusted. That's not the same as just saying, "I want more money." This is the difference between the employee who says, "What else can I do to make a contribution here; what else can I learn?" versus the person who says, "I'm having trouble making my mortgage payments, and my friends are earning more than I am."

• • •

In my own experience as a CEO, I'm looking for people who own what they do and who own the entire success of the organization. We're hungry for people who will come forward and say, "What more can I do?" This is not someone coming to me and saying, "I need more money because my car broke down or my kids are in college." The person needs to earn more, but the conversation instead is based on "How can I contribute more?"

Yes, those two conversations are entirely different. There are times when you need to have the money conversation with your boss, but it comes down to what's fair, what is the marketplace, and is your value being reflected properly. It's okay to have this conversation occasionally in your current job, and certainly when you are coming into a job from outside the company you are going to have this dialogue. In that case, the prospective employee would say something like, "It's my understanding that a person in this position should be paid X, and that's what I was expecting based on the contribution I would be making."

From a corporate standpoint, dealing with a person who has done the homework, knows the marketplace, and wants to be treated fairly is not a turnoff. This is a conversation that can be done with respect and the right attitude.

• • •

We've been talking about motivation and how people are perceived. One of the important things for people to know before they engage in the job search and negotiation process is how they come across. Too often, however, people don't invite feedback. One result of this is that they have views of themselves that are not particularly realistic. Or they may have the ten-

dency to oversell themselves and end up in jobs for which they were not qualified.

You've hit on an area that occurs regularly. I'll give you an example: A young woman I know, back in the days when "dot-com" was still fairly new, was able to convince people that she could do a job in this new venue. She had talent, skills, and experience that could be applied to this new job, but she did not totally understand what she was getting into. She found she had to work hard to learn many new things just to keep up with the expectations. It was very frustrating and highly stressful, to the point that she really questioned what she had gotten herself into and whether she should stay. Ultimately, she persevered and prevailed, and the experience was rewarding, but it could have been disaster.

The danger here is if you're good at promoting the best of your skills and you end up with a job for which you're really underqualified, then you will have to work doubly hard at it to make a contribution. That's a gamble that may or may not pay off.

There are also instances when this happens because of a miscommunication or misunderstanding between the candidate and the hiring manager related to the skill level that is required for the job. This typically happens in a new area for the company or in the marketplace. When this occurs, there are bound to be mismatches.

OVERSELLING, OVERPROMISING, AND UNDERDELIVERING

THE TRAP: You oversell yourself and get in over your head.

THE LESSON: I've seen countless examples of people who are excellent at selling themselves in the interview process and who have exaggerated their accomplishments and successfully convinced employers that they could perform at a higher level and accomplish more than they were capable of. The consequence? Some were fired, some were occasionally demoted, and many were dead-ended. They were seen as mediocre performers not worthy of consideration for advancement or promotion, let alone a raise in pay for making a valued contribution.

THE TIP: If you take a job that's a stretch for you, be confident that you can stretch into the job.

In other chapters we've discussed—from the employee's point of view—the importance of feedback and appraisals to make sure that there is an open dialogue with the manager about one's performance. Can you discuss appraisals from the other side?

Most managers hate to do appraisals and give feedback. When companies tie performance appraisals to compensation, it's a disaster. The employee just wants to get through the appraisal part to find out what the raise is going to be. The manager dreads the process, and the employee doesn't listen to anything except the bottom line.

Understanding this dynamic, employees who truly want feedback—and this is essential for ensuring that what you're working on is aligned with your boss's and your company's goals and priorities—should move the conversation off this unproductive cycle. Initiate an interactive conversation about your performance, keeping the boss informed about what you're doing and what you see as the next step and asking for guidance and input. This feedback on what you're doing and where you should be focusing will be most valuable to make sure your contribution is having the greatest impact.

• • •

What about when people are overqualified for a job? We have seen so much change in the job market. Senior people are becoming available who are overqualified for the job for which they are applying. They are good people, but there's a nagging question: Will this person be happy here? What are your thoughts?

You said it: There are various reasons why someone who is overqualified would be seeking an opportunity that is available. The key question is why. What is the reason that is driving them to do this? Did the person's previous job relocate, and they did not want to leave the area, and this is the only job that is available? Or did they not do as well in the previous job, and so they are not as successful as the skills they say they have would indicate? The answers to these questions are critical. The company is interested in people staying for the long term. It wants to minimize the turnaround because recruitment, selection, and training of new people are so costly.

Therefore, in situations with a candidate who appears to be overqualified, the company wants to know the real reason why the person is interested in this particular job. It could be that the person is willing to take a step back in order to move forward in a new area. For example, the person was in marketing before and had a relatively high-level position in that department but now wants to learn operations and is willing to take a step down in compensation and/or title and prestige in order to make that career transition. The person looks to be overqualified but wants to develop specific skills and experience, which—given that individual's track record—he or she could probably do very quickly.

• • •

A taboo subject in the job market is age. Yet age is a big factor in the job market right now given the aging of the baby boomers. We're also seeing the flattening of organizations with the removal of middle managers. So it's possible that there are many people in their fifties and sixties who are looking for work, and perhaps they are pursuing jobs for which they are perceived as being too old or too set in their ways. Or, a company may be concerned about hiring someone who is sixty because that person will not be with the organization long enough. There are many factors at work here, and yet there is a hunger for talent.

From the corporate standpoint, there are several factors to consider. One is that the corporation wants productivity and wants people to grow and be backups for the natural succession planning that all firms must have. They need an adequate number of people for this to occur—including a category of employees who are very productive but who are not looking to be upwardly mobile. For these reasons, there are companies that are willing to hire people who are toward the end of their careers, who are unlikely to move into higher-level jobs but who are quite productive.

In my industrial psychology class, we look at studies of demographics of the work force. The productivity of senior people is equal to the productivity of younger people because they know the shortcuts, not because they are more energetic. Older workers are good about showing up. Their attendance is very good—although there can be a slight deterioration in productivity because they may be ill a little bit more.

From a corporate standpoint, a company wants a high percentage of people who can be promoted and add value over the long haul. At the same time, many progressive companies also see the current demographics as an opportunity to broaden their work force and have senior people who can be good trainers.

•   •   •

If a job candidate is in his fifties, will he be considered based on who he is and what he can do, or is he at a disadvantage because he's not in his thirties and won't be at the company for the next thirty years? What advice would you have for someone like this?

From an organizational standpoint, if someone is fifty-five years old and wants to be challenged intellectually and wants to make a contribution, then how old that person is will not be an issue. A company wants a mix of young people who can be brought along in their careers. At the same time, if someone is fifty or fifty-five and has an attitude of ownership in the job and the organization, then a company wants this type of employee around. Also keep in mind that many baby boomers don't want to retire. They want to stay on in the work force a little while longer. If a person wants to contribute and can do that, age should be less of an issue. The employer wants to know if you are coasting, occupying a desk until the right job comes along, or if you really want to make a contribution in this new role.

•   •   •

In my twenty-five years of executive search, one of the unfortunate things I've found that can happen to some people as they get more experience is they become cynical and bitter and lose some of their initiative. This is not because someone is older; it is not related to age. On the other hand, it is no accident that the CEOs who are in their fifties and sixties are anything but

cynical and bitter. They are people who maintain and grow their desire to make a difference in the world. They have a mission and a purpose. They add wisdom, experience, and competency.

I believe what happens to some people as they get older is they have set unrealistic goals of becoming CEO or earning a pile of money, and when they get into their fifties these objectives seem out of range. These people are probably going to be cynical because they believe that something or someone else got them off track and prevented them from accomplishing their goals. However, there are other people who set their goals for happiness based on making a contribution and making a difference in other people's lives. They have balance in their lives and what makes them happy. Their goals tend to be more realistic and broad. When they're in their fifties and they're not CEO, they are not cynical. Some may seek outside experiences for gratification—for example, joining a nonprofit organization where they can become leaders. Happiness in one's career over the long term is all about setting goals and accepting where you can make a contribution.

From the company's standpoint it is difficult to deal with cynics because most of the source of this attitude is internal to the person and may not be job related at all. Employers typically don't want this type of person to stay around because it poisons the environment for others.

•   •   •

Another way that someone can make a contribution—especially at the six-figure-salary level—is by mentoring others. Can you speak to that?

During my career, we loved to hire people whose management style was to coach others and mentor them in the broad sense. Managers who can do that will also be looking for young people who are not in their departments but who may be in adjacent departments, whom they can help to move along. They will give these young people tips and advice: things that mentors do subtly but powerfully.

From the company's perspective, the most valuable six-figure person is one who develops more "six-figure people."

•   •   •

Let's talk specifically about someone making a six-figure salary. What advice would you give this person?

Up to about the $100,000 a year level, you are still compensated based on your "technical abilities," meaning how well you can perform the tasks and duties and carry out the responsibilities as an individual contributor. When you get to $150,000 to $200,000 a year, it's really about your ability to influence others in positive ways and being a change agent—not your technical abilities.

At some point in a manager's career—usually at the vice president level—raw talent and determined ambition become less important than the ability to influence. The higher up you are in compensation, the greater the requirement that you influence others both inside and outside the organization. The degree to which people succeed at this level—those who do better or worse than others—is almost always related to attitude and personality, not on technical competency. It's about interpersonal skills, influencing people, and being a change agent.

In my thirty-five years in the corporate world, I could always hire someone who could tell me what the problem was—in other words a good analyst or diagnostician. However, I could not find enough people who could implement changes and influence other people to work on what needed to be done and to accomplish the organization's goals. The more a candidate can demonstrate skills in being a change agent—a leader who can bring a team along to support the goals of an organization—the more that person can show that he or she will be the leader to help others to do things differently.

CHAPTER TEN

Being a Buyer, Not a Seller

with Bob Wright

Out of work and with his severance package coming to an end, Dave Jensen was in a panic, and all he could think about was getting a job. From his first conversation with the recruiter to his interviews with HR and the hiring manager and his follow-up conversations, all he focused on was how to get hired.

Dave Jensen was a seller—trying to sell himself to the highest bidder, or to any bidder for that matter.

As a seller, Dave was mired in fear and scarcity. He did not feel sufficiently confident or valuable to ask enough questions or the right questions in order to determine if this was the best working environment for him—or the right job within that company. Had he been a buyer, Dave would have engaged in the due diligence to find out as much as he could, while relying on a broad-based team of advisors to keep him on track.

Buyers are more successful negotiators when it comes to finding the right job and getting paid a six-figure salary. Being a buyer requires a challenging shift in attitude, thinking, and approach for most people. Instead of trying to "sell" the company on their talent, services, and labor, buyers ask in-depth questions and evaluate multiple opportunities in order to find the best position in which to invest their talent, skills, and experience. Being a buyer in the job market requires the same kind of discernment that a wise consumer uses when making significant purchases such as a house or a car. Buyers want to make the best possible choice to meet their needs. Car buyers have many options and choices, and need to be convinced that the car is right for them. Homebuyers weigh yet another even more complex set of variables from schools to lifestyle, transportation, and resale value.

Similarly, being a buyer in the interview process involves engaging in a combination of fact-finding and test-driving. Rather than trying to do anything and everything to convince the company to hire you, as a buyer you are focused on whether this is the next right opportunity for you. The problem, however, is that as soon as you really want a job or you are afraid that you're not going to get that job (or maybe any job), you lose the buyer perspective and become a seller—and sometimes a desperate one at that.

Being a buyer is easier said than done.

"I had the viewpoint that I *had* to get a job," Dave observed. "I never approached the job search process from the perspective that I was choosing, that I got to ask the questions. I didn't feel like a buyer. I was definitely a seller."

Being a buyer is not about arrogance or exhibiting a superior attitude. A buyer can be respectful, inquisitive, and genuinely interested in the opportunity. At the same time, being a buyer means that you're aware that a career change at the six-figure-salary level is a long-term relationship. If you stay at a job for three years, then at the $100,000 compensation level, you are buying a $300,000 product—namely, a position that will provide you with the challenges, learning opportunities, mentoring relationships, and more that you desire. With that kind of commitment, you want to make sure you're buying the right product.

"That would have been a total mind shift for me," Dave remarked. "I was just trying to make sure that I got a job that would pay me enough money. I never looked at it as an opportunity I was buying with my talent, skills, and experience."

Dave's experience is by no means unique. For most people there comes a point in the job negotiation process when they *want* a job so much that they spend all their energy trying to sell the company on why they should be hired—without thinking about why they should want to work for that company or in that position.

Bob Wright—an internationally recognized author, speaker, educator, top-level executive coach, program developer, and nationally recognized entrepreneur in his own right—advises that the best way to remain a buyer and to avoid the trap of becoming a seller is to surround yourself with advisors who will support and coach you to ask probing questions and undertake the necessary due diligence through the interview process.

Bob has spent more than thirty years developing his human performance businesses and training, coaching, and consulting with business clients from small entrepreneurial start-ups to *Fortune* 100 firms. The author of *Beyond Time Management: Business with Purpose* and *People Skills*, he currently runs the Wright Leadership Institute, as well as training and coaching national and international business leaders on business success, personal development, corporate growth, change, effectiveness, and leadership.

Known for his Integrative Comprehensive Model of Human Development, Bob has been recognized for his work around the globe. He has also founded and cofounded several grass-roots regional organizations focusing on human potential and environmental issues.

•　　•　　•

Let's talk about the thinking that most people have when they go into the job search and salary negotiation process.

The major fear that hits people is, "Will I get another job?" or, "Will I get the job I want?" People come in wanting a job, and so the question becomes, "Will I get the job or won't I get the job?" They don't come in wanting enough. The challenge is to want the right job or the best job for you.

Even if you already have a job, a lot of people are afraid to take the job they really want. One of our leadership trainees was the HR director of a very conservative firm, and he wanted desperately to get into a forward-thinking, innovative firm that would better use his talents and challenge him more. Next thing you know, he gets a job offer from a very forward-thinking firm that was everything he claimed to want. They would certainly have used his HR expertise better than his current firm ever dreamed of using it, but he was too afraid to take the job. He was afraid of finding out whether he was really the HR hotshot he thought he was or could be. He preferred staying in a firm that didn't expect as much out of an HR director, and fifteen years later, he's still with that firm.

$$\bullet \quad \bullet \quad \bullet$$

Fear keeps people from exploring opportunities and even considering what might be the best environment for them. Fear locks them into being sellers. Buyers are people who can ask probing questions despite their fears, questions that give them meaningful information.

Fear makes people stay in jobs, and fear makes people move into the wrong jobs. Not understanding themselves and not assessing situations as savvy buyers and instead being sellers causes people to make huge mistakes.

Too many people don't look for the best environment for themselves. They look to escape their current job and, as a result, move from one problem to the next. I guess we could say there are two kinds of people: There are people who are looking for a great place for themselves, and they have a picture of what that is, and there are people who are looking for the least bad place or just a different place.

I know from coaching people that they have to be buyers, not sellers. As a buyer you interview people better. As a buyer you think about what the implications are for you. As a buyer, you get higher-quality information. As a buyer you are more discerning.

Even if you puff yourself up, as a seller you are a beggar. As a seller, you look at the wrong things. As a seller you go in one down; you negotiate from a position of inferiority. As a buyer you go in one up; you move to a position of superior perspective that gives you greater information and insight. As a buyer, you have what they need and they need you. As a seller, they have what you want; they have the job and you need them. Sellers are more subjective, and buyers are more likely to be objective.

The whole point is to go in as a buyer and to realize that there are infinite possibilities for you—but there is only one you for them. However, just like that's not the attitude that people go into marriage with, it's not the attitude that they go into their jobs with. It causes marriages to fail, and it causes the majority of people to work at jobs they do not love.

Traps, Lessons, & Tips

GIVING INTO THE FEAR FACTOR

THE TRAP: Your fears undermine your attempts to engage in successful salary negotiation.

THE LESSON: As we've seen throughout this book with Dave Jensen's story, his fear of being unemployed hurt him in almost every aspect of salary negotiation. It caused him not to ask questions, not to value his strengths, and to undersell his capabilities. It also cost him a lot of money.

All of us have a choice between an attitude of abundance (meaning there is more than enough opportunities, money, resources, and so forth to go around) and one of scarcity. Choosing abundance empowers you to be a buyer and to maximize your giving and receiving. You are not afraid to ask questions, pursue opportunities, and to more fully engage in negotiation, because you understand that is part of the process.

THE TIP: Negotiate from abundance.

When people are in unhappy marriages or are unhappy in their jobs, they often see the grass as greener on the other side of the fence and think that if they were only in that different relationship or that different job that all their problems would be solved. Is this part of the seller mentality?

We do not always recognize our motivation. We often see the new job as a magical solution to problems we wish to escape. We make up stories and rationalizations that cover up lessons we need to learn at our current or past job. There are important questions to ask:

- What do we think we are escaping in going to the new job?
- What unfinished business will we carry?
- How are we unconsciously planning or avoiding lessons in the new job?

Most of us have seen the romance fade in dating and committed relationships. We have also seen the initial excitement over a new and different job fade as the dynamics of the current job become similar to those of previous positions. Knowing that the glow will fade and anticipating the reality is a buyer skill.

• • •

The problem is that when you have the attitude of being the seller, you create scarcity for yourself, look for the one magical solution, and then are disappointed when the bloom is off the rose. That's the self-fulfilling prophecy of the seller. So how do people shift to being buyers when they don't feel like a buyer inside, when they don't feel like they have a lot of options, and they don't feel valued and wanted?

There is always the "fake it 'til you make it" approach. You ask lots of questions, and you act like a buyer, even though inside you are dying, and you just want them to hire you. The other approach is to look at your self-esteem and really work until you feel good enough about yourself so that you would only accept a position or join a company that's really good for you.

• • •

So either you feel deserving to be a buyer or you act as if you feel deserving.

Most people have to act like they feel deserving. If you already have a job, that's easier. However, if you are unhappy with that job and you want to escape, it's going to be more difficult.

The more that you move into the seller position the more likely you are going to make a mistake, because as a seller, fear is dominating your interactions. Your fear of not having enough will cause you to make more compromises than are necessary and will lead you to miss out on the satisfaction available to you. It's like you are so afraid of having an empty glass that you fill it with brackish water.

• • •

The marriage metaphor really works here. You don't want to be desperate to find just anybody because you want to get married. You want the right relationship.

Interestingly, in the United States, where we have romantic marriage, 50 percent of the marriages fail. In places where there are arranged marriages—take India for example—the divorce rate is 4 percent or less. Why? In part because in arranged marriages the family does a better job of due diligence from the buyer's perspective than the individuals do on their own.

Here's some advice to help you be a buyer and not a seller in the job negotiation process: Have your own advisory group behind you, who knows you and knows what's good for you. In the job search process, you want to have your metaphoric family who is going to be looking out for your best interests and helping you to maintain a buyer's perspective. They will ask things about the possibilities for you in the job that will encourage you to deepen your inquiry into the position, company, and culture. They will ask the very hard questions about why the company is looking to hire someone.

A really good corporate interviewer is going to find out in-depth why you're looking. The question is, will you really find out why the company is looking? Who was in the job before? Was that person successful? Was that person beloved or reviled? Was that person valued, or was that person diminished?

You want to know what the culture is around that position: Do people expect that position to be successful, or do people expect it to be a failure? Your metaphoric family, your advisory group, is more apt to ask that kind of question than you are. That's not an obvious question that people who are looking for a job will ask.

•   •   •

As a buyer you remain skeptical enough to keep looking for the answers. As a seller, you aren't willing to look at things the way they are.

As a seller, you are acutely aware of your own limitations, and you try to present the best face you can. As a buyer, you want to be acutely aware of the corporation's strengths and weaknesses and find the best environment you can for yourself. The corporation will be selling you by telling you how good it is and why you should be there. But as a buyer, you are really going to be looking at the downside of that job and that corporation.

When you are a buyer, you have wealth, and you want to deploy that wealth. As a seller, you desperately want the wealth, and you want to make an exchange of yourself for that wealth. There is a self-fulfilling prophecy here. As a buyer, you are aware of your own wealth and your own value. The company that's interviewing you believes that you have wealth and you have value. As a result, they are more likely to pay you a higher salary and to make the agreements and the concessions that you need in order for it be a good environment for you.

On the surface, it's very straightforward, but in practice it's much, much harder because the minute we get face-to-face with people, we tend to become sellers.

•   •   •

Why is that?

We want to be accepted. The desire to be accepted causes us to act in ways that we think will cause us to be accepted, rather than to act in ways that cause us to be skeptical and to measure more—

especially in the United States. In this country, we are very heavily into exchanging signs of acceptance.

•   •   •

So we ask, "Do you accept me?" rather than "Do I accept you?" Also, the real issue is not acceptance, but rather, is this a good relationship and a good fit?

Buyers who are interviewing for a job ask to meet a whole host of people in the company to gauge the fit. Some companies want you to meet a bunch of people, but do sellers think about which people they want to interview? No. As a seller, you just want them to give you a job! When you transform into a buyer, then you want a much broader picture of the company. You want to interview people, and you are going to ask very hard questions, including how many people have been in this position.

•   •   •

The analogy that comes to mind is selling a car versus buying a car. When you are selling a car, you don't care all that much about the details. You just want to do the transaction and get the money. But if you're buying a car, there is a lot of information that you want.

That's a great metaphor. When you're buying a car, you want to know all sorts of things: the repair record, the mileage, the durability, the features and functionality, what *Consumer Reports* says about it. . . .

Just as with the buyer of a car who is looking at different models, when you're a buyer in the job market you should be comparing multiple options. The problem, however, is that people want to get things over with so they don't create enough abundance. The successful buyer wants to know what's out there. The successful buyer really wants to compare and contrast options to get what is best for them.

• • •

Can you give me an example?

Here's one: A senior manager was earning $160,000 to $200,000 working for a high-tech company owned by a private equity firm that was having difficulty. He was let go and found himself in the job market. As he interviewed with a number of companies, you could watch him go from being a buyer to being a seller.

To remain a buyer you should be comparing multiple options. In this situation, what happened was that he would get a good job possibility, then he would stop calling, stop talking to people, and start hoping. Finally I was able to get through to him that at any given moment he should have a minimum of four good possibilities so that he would have that sense of abundance. Eventually he expanded his possibilities to eight, and that made a dramatic difference.

FOCUSING ON ONE OPPORTUNITY

THE TRAP: You put all your eggs in one basket.

THE LESSON: When in the job market it is almost always better to have multiple good opportunities available to you. In doing so, you will be operating from abundance rather than scarcity. You will be able to contrast and compare strengths and weaknesses and be in a stronger negotiating position for the opportunities you desire.

THE TIP: Actively pursue multiple opportunities.

. . .

We all have the tendency—even though we know what's right for us—that as soon as we decide we want something, we get caught up and shift from being a buyer to being a seller.

That's why you want to have advisors, to help you stay in that buyer's mode. They'll keep asking you the questions and keep orienting you to a buyer's perspective, so you won't fall into a selling perspective. Another key element is to make sure your advisors are people who know you and understand you and who also have insight into corporations and cultures. You also want to make sure there is someone on your team who understands the industry you're in or various industries if you are looking across several. There is just a basic fact that certain corporations are in growth industries and are more likely to be exploding while others are in dying industries and are contracting.

. . .

Here's another example: A man has made some mistakes in his current position and therefore perceives that he has a limited future in that organization. Through an ex-colleague, another company contacts him, and he interviews there. Because of what has happened in his current position he acts as a seller and not a buyer. When he's offered a lateral move, he starts looking for reasons to accept it just to get out of his current position.

That gets us into another complex issue, which is why self-knowledge is so important, and why understanding and analyzing your situation and your circumstances is really useful. In this example, we're talking about someone whose fear is causing him to want to escape, and he doesn't care where he escapes to. He convinces himself that he has a limited future, so he's perfectly happy to take a lateral move because he thinks he can't move up where he is, which may not have been true. If he had advisors around him, they would have helped him see the situation in the proper context, so that he could have seen the different possibilities.

•   •   •

A lot of people are in that position: They don't consider themselves valuable enough to go out and see that they do have value to offer.

People tend to overestimate or underestimate skills and attributes. Most people are in that situation. That is why the advisory team is so important. It's the same with dating. It's rare that someone has enough self-esteem and enough drive to really have a great relationship. They settle, rather than exploring what is possible. The same thing holds true for a career. The compelling question then becomes, "How do I develop the self-esteem," which we really can't address here. For our purposes, fake it until you make it, and have your advisors help. Set up some way to pull off being a buyer rather than a seller. Create a committee of advisors, and let them know that it's their job to cover your blind spots and to help you do the due diligence.

As a buyer, you must undertake due diligence the same way an investment firm does when analyzing an investment—only more. Not only do you want to know the balance sheet and the profit and loss statement of the company but also the culture, how it values people, how it develops people, how it moves people, how it rewards people. The chapters in this book cover all the questions you should ask. You could take each one of the chapters and assign it to someone on your committee, who would then own that one question. One advisor has retirement, another compensation, someone else value.

• • •

One of the reasons we need other people is what I call "de facto justification," which is how we make up reasons for things to justify an emotional response. Once I like something, I make up all sorts of reasons why it's the right thing for me. I pretend that I'm a buyer, but I'm really a seller.

This falls under the heading of "traps and errors to watch out for," or "how to sniff out your own b.s.," because that's just what you outlined. Here's another case study for you: A woman hates her job. She thinks her boss is domineering, and she hasn't been willing to stand up to him, so she wants to escape that job. A friend tells her about another job, and she falls in love what that job. When she does, she puts the blinders on. However, she pretends to do the due diligence, building a case for that other job. People do this all the time: They fall in love with the retirement plan, or the boss, or whatever, and they don't really look at who they are.

In this case study, this woman has not been willing to stand up to her boss. She thinks she's not appreciated in the current company. Then somebody tells her about another company, and she meets someone from that company who thinks she's great. She makes it up in her head that this is a much better company: The people are more accepting there, and they are really going to appreciate her gifts. Next thing you know, she's in the exact same bind she was in before—she's not standing up for herself enough to really move ahead in the new company.

BEWARE YOUR PERSONAL PITFALLS

THE TRAP: You trip over your unconscious barriers.

THE LESSON: We all have unconscious behavior patterns and habits that interfere with making the most of our contribution and our compensation. These include such things as procrastination, underselling yourself, not listening well, exaggerating, not working your hardest, not appreciating yourself, and so on. There are measurable consequences to acting out of these fears and habits. For example, if you are afraid to ask for what you want, you are less likely to get it. By understanding your individual potential pitfalls and by using your support team's help and feedback, you can plan and act in ways to maximize your success. This is particularly true for the negotiation process.

THE TIP: Know your own personal traps.

Consider this example: A man has a very successful career as a consultant with a great future ahead of him, but he decides that he wants the more sexy business world of investment banking. So he's interviewed by a company to handle mergers and acquisitions. He falls in love with this idea and doesn't do the due diligence about the company or the boss who is hiring him. He doesn't talk to the board. Instead he jumps firms. Inside of a month, he's calling his former boss and asking whether he can go back to his old job. This is a guy who is very intelligent, very successful, and has a wealthy family behind him, but because of his fantasies about what he wants he instantly becomes a seller. He doesn't do any due diligence on the job at

all—which is ironic, since his whole job is to do due diligence (in a different arena.)

The problem with being a seller is you sell yourself. You often cease looking objectively. As a buyer you are much more likely to do the due diligence. Now, can you in the extreme become too much of a buyer and not move? Yes. But the greater danger is becoming a seller and not doing enough due diligence or none at all.

• • •

Let's go further with the case of people with low self-esteem and who have to "fake it until they make it." What are some good, buyer-type questions to ask in the midst of the interview?

Here's one: Why don't you have somebody already for this position? That teases out a host of questions that don't get asked.

Who was in this job before? How long was that person in the job? How well did they do the job? Where are they now?

If they didn't get a promotion, why aren't they there? If they did get a promotion, why didn't you have someone there already? These questions tell you a whole lot about the culture.

Another buyer approach: I'd like to interview the most honest person close to this job who will tell me the pluses and minuses of the position and the company.

Or, what's it like if I disagree with you as the boss? How do directives come down in the company?

There are so many questions about how a company operates that don't get asked very often.

The thing that sellers do, which buyers do not, is that sellers want to close the deal right way. Real buyers get to see what the firm is made of because they are not in a hurry.

•   •   •

Let's turn the tables. What does it feel like for an employer to be on the receiving end of those buyer questions?

First of all, as the employer if you are feeling relatively secure in yourself and your organization, you will feel slightly uneasy at being asked these questions, and you will respond truthfully to give the candidate a realistic sense of the opportunity. If you are insecure about yourself and the organization, you will feel more fearful and defensive. Once the manager gets over the fear, the issue is: What does this question tell me about this person? Most managers are impressed.

A lot of it depends on the person. I had a prospective candidate ask me recently about budget and growth plans, and I didn't have great specifics. I told her, "I don't think we have the plans that you're looking for." Then she said, "That interests me, because I can play a major role in developing them." My security allowed me to give an honest answer in the face of fear of rejection and, instead, I received a resounding yes vote.

•   •   •

I recently interviewed a woman who was a fairly senior consultant. During the interview, she asked what seemed to be buyer's questions, but she did so in such a superior way that she made me feel as if there was something wrong with me and my company. I have since learned that this is a problem she has had elsewhere as well.

In her case, she was faking it. She was trying to appear knowledgeable by making you feel inadequate, when the fact of the matter was she was implying a substance beyond what she had. She wasn't being a buyer. As a buyer, you are negotiating as you ask questions.

As a seller you are begging someone to negotiate with you. She was really doing neither. She was trying to intimidate.

• • •

As a buyer, you're asking genuine questions to tease out more information, not to show off what you know.

That's right. You shouldn't ask questions if the answers are ones you're not prepared to process, digest, and interact with—or at least go back to your advisors and let them help you with the next level.

I don't think we can underline enough the importance of having advisors. It takes a lot more security to have advisors. Paradoxically, secure people assuage their insecurity with advisors. Insecure people deny their insecurities and go it alone.

• • •

It's not just insecurity. If I am a seller and I'm in such scarcity that I think this is the only opportunity I have, I won't bring in advisors.

No, because you're afraid that someone will kill the deal by telling you something that you don't want to hear.

• • •

What is your advice for people who don't have advisors and want to know how to go about finding them?

Part of the bind is you should have mentors already, and you should already have an advisory board. Work is like sports. Top athletes always have coaches, and top performers at work generally have advisors. If you don't have them yet, then you need to take a good hard look at your career, and you need to take a good hard look at your life team. If your life team doesn't have those advisors, then step one is you can hire one. Make sure it's someone good. Top coaching pays for itself many times over. If you're in a specific field, hire a head-hunter, not to get you a job, but to advise you. Interview headhunters the same way, as a buyer. Find someone and pay her on an hourly basis to be your advisor. Ask her who else can help. Pick the highest level of people among your family and friends. Your advisors have to be people who understand the complexity of what you're doing.

Your Advisory Team

To successfully negotiation your next job offer and salary package, you are going to need help. For some people this can be a challenge, either because they want the bragging rights that they did it all themselves, or they are afraid that others' feedback will make an opportunity look less than promising. Your advisory team's most important role is to help you remain a buyer—looking at every opportunity with discernment and without the desperation of becoming a "seller" to get the company to hire you. With an advisory team behind you, it's far more likely that you will feel confident and empowered from the first interview through the salary negotiation and to job acceptance.

Further, your advisory team can assist you in asking the right questions—the ones that will uncover additional information that you need to make the best decision for you. Rather than focusing only on one or two aspects of the job, asking buyer's questions will help you see the complete package, from salary to benefits to corporate culture to career path.

This exercise has two parts:

- Putting together your Advisory Team
- Putting together your buying questions

YOUR ADVISORY TEAM

Just as a company has a Board of Advisors, put together your own personal board to advise you on your job search and negotiation. For each of the areas described below, ask someone to be your advisor on the subject:

Your strengths: _____

_____

Your weaknesses: _____

_____

Lessons learned at current and past jobs: _____

_____

Lessons left to learn: _____

_____

Corporate culture in your prospective employer: _____

_____

Compensation: _____

_____

Benefits: _____

_____

Strengths and weaknesses of the organization and its industry:

_____

_____

The value you offer the organization: _____

_____

The value the opportunity offers you: _____

_____

BUYER QUESTIONS TO ASK

Put together a list of questions that buyers would ask if they had an abundance of opportunities before them. Imagine the attitude of wealthy car buyers who have many vehicles from which to choose and are asking questions to determine what is the best car for them. Here are some examples of buying questions from this chapter:

■ Why don't you already have somebody for this position?

■ Who was in this job before? How long was that person in the job? How well did he or she do the job? Where is that person now?

■ If he or she didn't get a promotion, why did that person leave? If he or she did get a promotion, why didn't you have someone ready to take this position?

■ I'd like to interview the most honest person close to this job who will tell me the pluses and minuses of the position and the company.

■ What's it like if I disagree with you as the boss? How do directives come down in the company?

CHAPTER ELEVEN

Negotiating Your Offer

Y ou may come to the negotiation process through a number of different circumstances. Like Dave Jensen, you may have to negotiate for a new position because you've suddenly lost your job as a result of restructuring or downsizing by your former employer. You may be recruited for a position at another company. Or, you may decide that it's time to take a new challenge elsewhere with a different position, either internally within your company or with another employer. No matter what the reason or circumstance, there are some common threads and approaches that apply. In previous chapters, CEOs and top professionals in their fields have shared valuable perspectives, advice, and experiences regarding the most critical aspects of the negotiation and hiring process. The objective has been to help you obtain a win for you and a win for the organization. Now, it's time to bring it all together and underline the lessons learned.

Lessons from the Masters

In every chapter, themes were repeated and affirmed—for example, the importance of being prepared, asking the right questions, considering the fit with the corporate culture, and so forth. Now let's take these lessons one at a time for a deeper look.

Salary Negotiation Is Like Courtship and Marriage

In the employment arena, just as in matters of the heart, it's either win/win or lose/lose. It does neither party—in this case neither you nor the company—any good if one feels victorious and the other defeated. If you get more money than you deserve, there is a good likelihood that it will damage your prospects in the future. You may even be terminated because you are not able to deliver what you were expected to, given the level of compensation that you're receiving. Similarly, if it appears that the company was victorious and has been able to get you "on the cheap," you will remain dissatisfied and be more likely to leave when you come across an opportunity in which you perceive you are being treated more fairly.

Your objective and the organization's objective should be that you *both* win.

Go for Fairness

This is the high ground to which you can continually orient, bringing both points of view into alignment. You and the company can work together to find a solution that you each find acceptable. While fairness is a subjective concept, both parties will agree that the objective is to negotiate whatever is fair.

Do Your Homework

Every expert interviewed in this book talked about the importance of gathering data and intelligence in their particular area of expertise. For example, you should understand the salary and compensation structure of your current organization and the company with which you are negotiating, as well as the general market for your profession and your field. Analyze the benefits package in your current job and the benefits being offered by the organization with which you are negotiating. Regarding corporate culture, ask questions and meet with people outside your prospective chain of command, and understand everything you can about how work is done, how decisions are made, and every aspect of the corporate culture that you can explore.

Ask Questions

Dave Jensen did not ask enough questions to enable him to get crucial information that would have helped him do a better job of getting the job and the compensation he deserved. In some cases, he would have received information that would have made him more enthusiastic. In others, information would have influenced his negotiation; for example, he would have been led to ask for more vacation time—or even a higher-level job.

Trust and Verify

In general, during the hiring process you will be more successful and set yourself up better in the organization if you assume goodwill on the part of the people with whom you are negotiating. Operate on the basis that they want to treat you fairly. They are interested in you contributing the most that you can, and they want to reward you for your contribution.

The other side of trust is to verify. Trust is not blind. In other words, assume goodwill, but get it in writing. If they say wonderful things about the organization, confirm it with independent sources; don't just rely on what the manager says. What do their vendors say? What do their customers say? What do people who used to work there say? What do the administrative assistants in the company say? Use multiple sources of information to ensure that what you're being told is accurate.

Show How You Can Contribute and Add Value

At its most elemental level, compensation should be commensurate with the value received. The more you contribute to the company, the more the company will want to pay you. The more giving you are, the more you will be given. Also keep in mind that at the six-figure salary level, part of your contribution is not just what *you* can do but how you can help others maximize their contribution.

In the example of Dave Jensen's job negotiation, one of the consequences of his not asking enough questions was that he didn't realize how his managerial skills would be valuable to the company. Had he known and demonstrated that value, he would have enhanced his ability to contribute to the organization. He probably received less compensation because he did not communicate that value to the organization. And why should the company have paid him more if they did not know he could contribute more?

Be a Buyer as Well as a Seller

When job candidates operate out of emotional scarcity, they are just "selling" themselves to the company. This often prevents them from being a "buyer," that is, asking the questions that will help them learn whether they want the job in the first place.

Once again, this happened with Dave Jensen. It was exacerbated in his case because he was unemployed, and he was operating out of scarcity because his severance was coming to an end, and he needed the income. He was selling himself and looking for someone who would quickly buy his labor. From his position, he was afraid that if he asked the wrong questions, they wouldn't buy and offer him the job. That attitude may have very well cost him thousands of dollars.

Being a buyer means that you're discerning about whether the job, the company, the manager, and the culture are right for you. You have value that you are going to give to whatever organization you choose. You are buying that opportunity and your compensation with your labor and your contribution.

It Is Your Job to Pursue Your Satisfaction

Your satisfaction is your responsibility. It is your job to analyze the situation and determine what you need to be satisfied. If things are not to your liking, it's your job to either change your attitude or change your situation. Whether the issue is salary, job duties, benefits, who your manager is, or how well you are recognized for what you accomplish, you are responsible for yourself.

Salary and Bonus Are but One Small Part of Value

As Stan Smith expressed so well in Chapter 2, value includes many things other than money. It also includes factors such as who mentors you and whom you mentor, what you learn, and how you increase your competencies. Value also includes how you help others to be more effective and improve their skills and competencies. Flextime and travel time are part of the value equation. All these elements need to be taken into account in considering what you're giving and what you're receiving in relation to your work.

Put Compensation in Its Proper Place

Compensation is the last thing to be negotiated. Not only is that the right time in the ebb and flow of the negotiation process, it also communicates to the hiring manager that you are interested first and foremost in this being the right opportunity for you. And, of course, you understand that you will be appropriately rewarded for the contribution that you make to the organization.

If a company tells you the salary for the job upfront, and if it's below what is acceptable to you, it is often effective to respond with questions. For example, "Can you tell me what the grade level is for this position and what the salary range is for this grade level?" Remember, in many organizations some employees are paid outside the salary range for their grade, although you will most likely have to demonstrate your contribution to the hiring manager so that he or she will convince the decision-makers to make an exception in your case.

Another strategy if the company brings up salary at the beginning is to say, "Let's talk about the opportunity first." One of things that may happen, once you are in the interview process, is that other opportunities may surface. Once they meet you and see the value that you will bring to the organization, company hiring managers may find other jobs in the organization for which you are better suited. They may even create a position for you.

The Five Key Principles of Job Negotiation

Five principles underlie the concepts in this book. They are the key foundational concepts of successful job negotiation and are operating principles for the development of your career. These five principles are:

1. **Truth:** If both sides tell the truth, then the right thing will tend to happen. If you have to lie to get a position, it is probably not the right position for you. If the company has to lie to get you, you're probably not the right person for them.

2. **Fairness:** As we've already discussed, focusing on fairness will tend to lead to optimal win/win negotiations.

3. **Attraction:** As job candidates, we want organizations to want us. The more they want us, and the more they think we want them, the more generous they are going to be—and the more they will go out of their way to try to attract us. This includes salary, bonus, benefits, opportunities, challenges, and future promotions.

4. **Contributing value:** Every organization is hungry for people who contribute their gifts and their talents to help the organization achieve its mission. And the more people give and they more they contribute, the more they are recognized and rewarded.

5. **Fit:** Just as you shouldn't go into a marriage with the expectation that your partner is going to change, do not go into an organization expecting the company to change so that you are more satisfied. (The one exception here is if you are hired as CEO with an explicit directive to change the company and its culture.) Your job as a buyer in the interview and negotiation process is to understand the organization and its culture as well as you possibly can to determine if the organization and its culture is a good fit for you, your talent, your personality, and your desires.

Know What You Can Negotiate

Early on in my executive search career, I came across a sign at a photocopying business: "Never teach a pig to sing. It wastes your time and annoys the pig." It's a funny saying that conveys a big truth: You have to know what can be done and what's a waste of time. People are annoyed when you waste their time. This is especially important in job negotiation. There are things that can be negotiated, and there are others that cannot. The problem for most job candidates is that they don't know the rules of the game. As a result, they are afraid of asking for the wrong thing, and they don't address things that are negotiable.

The following list contains elements of a job and job offer that are all potentially negotiable. This does not mean that in every situation all of these things are negotiable. However, you will not know unless you ask.

What to Negotiate

- Salary
- Bonus
- Vacation

- Signing bonus
- Timing of the first salary review
- Timing of promotion
- Training and education dollars
- Opportunities and projects
- Stock options

Tips for Successful Negotiation

No book on salary negotiation would be complete without a "tips" section on how to handle specific situations that come up in the interview process. The following tips are based on my experience as an executive recruiter, interviewing people for positions within my company, and interviewing with prospective clients and employers.

These tips relate to your mental preparation for the job interview, which begins as soon as you enter the job market. The better prepared you are in advance by doing your homework, collecting and analyzing data, and engaging in self-reflection, the more successful you are likely to be in the job interview and negotiation process.

Be Prepared to Answer Questions You're Likely to Be Asked

This first tip directly relates to your preinterview preparation. As your first interview approaches, you will want to have answers to questions that you can count on being asked. Some questions— including the ones in this list—are common to all candidates. Others are going to be triggered by your own unique experience, your previous position, or information you've disclosed on your resume.

Let's say that you've recently moved from Alaska to Atlanta, as reflected in your resume. Your last job was in Alaska, and now here you are in Atlanta. In this instance, you can count on someone asking why you moved. Knowing that, you would want to be prepared to answer that question in a way that is truthful and also presents you in a positive light.

One of the most revealing resumes of sorts I've ever encountered—which was sure to draw all sorts of questions from prospective employers—was published in the "Employment Wanted" section of the classified ads for the Toronto *Financial Post* in February 2001. The ad was placed by a former marijuana smuggler who had completed a ten-year sentence and had become a public service speaker to children and parents on the danger of drugs, which he said had earned him the praise and recognition of the Royal Canadian Mounted Police. His detailed business experience included owning and operating a multivessel fishing business, an island, and a processing facility; employing 120 people worldwide; and operating a venture that had more than $100 million in revenues annually. His attributes included being an expert in "all levels of security," with extensive computer skills and an outgoing personality.

One can only wonder what happened to this individual, who "took responsibility for my own actions" and listed references from "friends, family, and the U.S. district attorney." The interview question-and-answer session must have been fascinating!

The questions you're likely to face will also reflect your background (presumably in a legitimate line of work). If you've been in sales, you can expect questions that relate to your particular experience: What was your territory? Did you have a sales quota? How did you perform against that quota? How did your performance compare with other sales representatives? Similarly, if you are a candidate for a management position in operations, you can be expected to answer questions related to your accomplishments. To present yourself in the best light, you'll want to be prepared with answers and examples.

Beyond the questions specific to your background, there are a number of common queries that any candidate for any position should be prepared to answer. Here are a few examples:

What are your strengths?

The rule of thumb for addressing the topic of your strengths is that you should have at least two stories that demonstrate the benefit to the organization that accrues from a gift, talent, or other strength on your part. Let's say that initiative is one of your strengths. You know that everyone is looking for employees who take initiative. In order to present yourself in the best way possible, you should be prepared to tell a story about how your organization benefited from your initiative.

In his position as a sales manager for the manufacturer of precision plastic parts, sold mostly to the aerospace industry, Steve took the initiative to find new markets for the company's products. As part of his market research, he learned that the medical diagnostics industry required a similar level of precision for its parts. He took the initiative to contact twenty medical diagnostics companies, which resulted in a new market for the company. When Steve interviews for his next job, you can bet he'll tell that story as he illustrates how his employer benefited directly from his initiative.

When you talk about strengths, remember that your interviewers want to know how your particular talent, ability, or other attribute benefited the company, so make sure your stories relate to the value you bring. Your "strength" may be the ability to bench-press 300 pounds, but unless your job is demonstrating fitness equipment for bodybuilders, it's not going to be relevant for a job in which the greatest physical demand will be tapping a keyboard or clicking a mouse with your fingers. However, if your strength is problem solving, then by all means talk about it as it related to your last job when the company was facing a problem.

Donna was responsible for sales in the western region, where the company had experienced steady annual increases in revenue. When sales declined for the first time in five years, however, Donna suddenly found herself under pressure from the corporate office to find out what was happening. She analyzed the situation, looked at the numbers, and talked to salespeople in the field and to customers. The cause of the problem, she realized, was the closure of a customer service center in the region, which required salespeople to do more administrative work and spend less face-time with customers.

It took six months for corporate to take up the issue and get it resolved, but Donna's problem-solving ability was instrumental in uncovering the cause and implementing a solution. Once more administrative help was hired, and sales reps were able to spend more time with customers, sales increased again and exceeded previous levels. As Donna discusses her problem-solving abilities in her next interview for a job—whether inside the company or at another firm—you can be sure she will relate this story.

In both examples, interviewers are not only interested in hearing more about Steve's initiative and Donna's problem solving; they also want to think about how these strengths will benefit their company (or division or team, in the case of an internal opportunity).

Describe your weaknesses.

The weakness question is a tricky one because no one wants to showcase what they're bad at or how they need development out of fear that prospective employers could be turned off by the truth. (The generally accepted answers, as stated in Chapter 1, include "I'm really bad at work/life balance—I just work too much!" and "I'm too impatient with people who aren't as committed or competent as I am.")

That having been said, in my opinion it's better to give the example of a real weakness, provided that you can also demonstrate that you are working to improve or that you have figured out how to compensate for it. For example, a candidate might admit to being chronically five minutes late for meetings. To correct this problem, he has set up a system with a friend; every time he's not on time for a meeting, he pays $5. The consequences he has voluntarily set up are helping him overcome a bad habit.

This type of disclosure accomplishes several things. First, it demonstrates a level of honesty and genuineness on the part of the candidate. Second, it shows the interviewer the applicant's commitment to improvement, using creativity and initiative to solve problems and get results. Interviewers will be more impressed by a weakness that someone is working to improve than by the pretense that a person has no weaknesses.

Why are you interested in this opportunity?

The subtext for this question is "why do you want to leave your current situation?" The best way to answer this question is with a truthful explanation that combines current circumstances and the prospective opportunity.

Ben's current employer was well known to have been in crisis mode for many years, with news about its downsizing and closing or selling off divisions in the business media. When asked why he wanted to pursue a new opportunity, Ben referred to what was already known about his current employer and admitted, "It's not an enjoyable place to work." Then, addressing the prospective opportunity, Ben added, "From everything I've heard about this company, you're growing. You're looking for motivated people who can take this company to the next level, and that's the kind of opportunity I'm looking for."

Nobody wants to hire someone whose *sole* motivation is leaving an unhappy situation. Companies want to attract and hire people who are looking to be challenged, to grow, and to make a bigger contribution. Think back to the courtship analogy in the introduction to this book and liken the interview process to two people who are dating. If the only reason for pursuing a new relationship is because your last romance was bad, then what does that say? Romantic partners want to know why each is interested in the other—not just how bad some other relationship was. Now, that's not to say that questions won't come up about why someone broke off a long-term relationship or a marriage ended. But the focus is on the other person in the new relationship, not on how good it was to bail out of a bad one.

Even though you're in the midst of the job interview process, it could be that you're perfectly happy in your current situation; however, the new opportunity is your ultimate dream. If that's the case then say so. In general, present a combination of reasons regarding your current circumstances and why you are interested in this new opportunity.

How much money are you looking for?

In general, it is better *not* to put forth a number. Instead, you can say, "I'm looking for fair compensation in return for the value that I will contribute to the organization."

What are your biggest accomplishments?

Here is your opportunity to describe your contribution to your current employer—and how you expect to make a contribution in the new position. Be prepared to tell stories that exemplify your most critical competencies in action, whether taking initiative, being innovative, being a good team member, solving problems, being a good communicator, being results oriented, or being good at influencing others.

If an interviewer can grasp your proficiency in these key competencies, you will likely be wanted. If an interviewer doesn't think that you're a candidate for the position you are pursuing, your competencies make it far more likely that someone will look around for a different position in the company for which you are better suited.

Jane's company went through a major contraction that resulted in the elimination of her position as vice president of human resources, which carried a salary of $200,000 a year. She interviewed at a company that was ten times the size of her previous employer for the position of head of HR of a major division. The company decided to hire an internal candidate for that job. However, the head of HR for the entire company was so impressed by Jane that she asked recruiters to find out if Jane would be willing to work for the company for six months. During that time, Jane would learn the operations, and the right job would be found for her. In other words, Jane demonstrated so much competence in the interview process that the company was willing to hire her "on the bench" until an opportunity arose for her.

Negotiate in person whenever possible.

You are more likely to have a genuine interaction with the interviewer, and people are more likely to be generous with you if you talk in person. When you are face-to-face with other people, they can see your body language and what it says about your desire to join the company.

I have gotten many sales simply because I've gone out of my way to be face-to-face with someone, even when everything could easily have been said over the phone. Just recently I called a prospective client and offered to come to his office. When he assured me it wasn't necessary, I replied that I wanted to make the trip. We sat down and talked in person, and I walked away with a piece of business that came out of an off-handed conversation, which would not have transpired over the phone. The same kinds of things happen in the interview process.

At the Interview

Your preparation time is over. The day of the interview has arrived. Here are some important tips that will help you put your best foot forward.

When in doubt, overdress.

You don't want to show up in business casual for an interview when everyone else is in more formal business attire. If the opposite occurs, your prospective employer will know that you dressed to impress and to show respect.

You do not, however, want to do what Peter did. Now in his thirties, Peter recently received his MBA from one of the most prestigious business schools in the country. As a favor to his father, who is a top executive at one of the largest banks in the country, I interviewed Peter. When he came in to see me at my office, he wore a sport shirt and casual slacks—no doubt thinking that since I'm a friend of his father's he didn't have to dress up. But there I was in a suit and tie while Peter was dressed casually.

Personally, I don't care how somebody dresses, but it does tell me a lot about who they are. In Peter's case, the way he dressed that day told me he had not planned for the contingency of meeting someone else that day or what the situation might be. In fact, the CEO of a compensation consulting firm happened to be in my office that day, and I wanted him to meet Peter. Unfortunately, Peter damaged his prospects considerably by his choice of attire. To his credit, he did send me a note apologizing on his behalf and for embarrassing his father. However, he couldn't undo the damage he had caused for himself.

Don't be late.

That's an obvious one. Everybody knows that, right? Well, many years ago I was looking for a college graduate to hire as an assistant and to train in my business. I went to the best schools in Chicago and found an excellent candidate at the University of Chicago. I set up an interview with him—and he showed up twenty minutes late. He had a good excuse based on public transportation, and I gave him the benefit of the doubt. However, when he was late for the second meeting as well, that was it. He wasn't hired.

If an employer can't count on you showing up for an interview, how can anyone count on you being on time for the job and for meetings with clients? The rule of thumb for interviews is to show up early. Ten minutes ahead of time is sufficient.

Use humor.

Potentially tense or difficult conversations can be made much easier with humor. For example, the interviewer asks, "How much are you looking for in terms of salary?" You reply with a smile, "Well, I'd like a million dollars for the first six months, and then six months of vacation. . . . Seriously, I'm looking for fair compensation for what I'm going to contribute."

In my business, I aim to use humor in almost every sales transaction and with clients to establish rapport, build warmth, and to put us both on the same side of the table.

If you don't know how to answer a question, ask a question to get more information.

Let's say the interviewer asks you how much money you're looking for. Typically you don't know how to answer because you don't have enough information. So you ask a question: "Is there a defined salary range for this position?" Or, you are asked if you'd be willing to travel. You can ask, "Does the position require much travel?" Often interviewers pose the wrong questions, meaning they don't ask in a way that will get them answers that are relevant to the real issues involved.

Take the example of "Are you willing to travel?" Let's say that you have two young children and you don't want to travel much. However, it's also not true that you can't (or won't) travel at all. Therefore, if you ask, "Does the job require a lot of travel?" you will be given more information that helps you answer the question truthfully—and discern if this position is right for you. The interviewer tells you, "The job requires a three-day trip once every two months for a sales meeting. Is that something you can do?" Having asked the right question, you can give an honest answer.

Don't repeat the question.

Repeating a question that's just been asked is perceived as an inelegant stall tactic to buy time to figure out a "correct" response. It does not leave a positive impression. A better tactic is to be silent for a moment and think about the question. If you don't understand the question, say so, and ask about what you don't understand.

Use silence where appropriate.

This doesn't just apply to questions you need to ponder for a moment, but it is also an important part of your negotiation tactics. Anybody who has ever negotiated a deal knows that there are situations in which the person who speaks first loses. Often, silence builds anxiety, and people talk to relieve the tension. Learn to live with tension, and you will be more successful in negotiation.

Get it in writing.

Companies sometimes make verbal promises that never materialize for any number of reasons. Mary's old boss from two employers back had moved on, becoming chief operating officer (COO) for a well-known midsized company. She contacted Mary and asked her to interview for a position. At the interview, Mary's former boss told her great things about the company, including future opportunities. However, Mary would first have to take a lateral job, then in six months, when the right opportunity opened up, Mary would be promoted. Mary accepted the job and started working; two weeks later her former boss, the COO, was fired.

Two years later, Mary has still not been promoted. She has no evidence that she was promised a promotion in six months. Get it in writing. (This is a corollary of the principle "Trust and verify.") If they won't put it in writing, don't count on it happening.

I've seen people misled by promises that others won't put in writing, offering one excuse or another for not doing so. Most often, however, things aren't put in writing because people don't ask for it. So ask.

Whenever possible negotiate with the line decision-maker instead of HR.

As we've discussed at several points in this book, human resources is more likely to want to adhere to a firm policy, while line managers are more willing to push for exceptions to pay outside of a salary range in order to hire someone they really want.

I recently spoke to a woman who described to me a situation that was not as uncommon as you might think. She had been recruited for a senior professional position in an organization and was negotiating with HR. The department would not change its position over salary and flextime. As a result, she did not take the job that otherwise would have been a great position for her. Six months later, she was at a reception at a conference where she saw the manager for whom she would have been working at the company. He asked her what happened—why hadn't she taken the job? He listened and then asked with amazement, "Why didn't you call me?" Her response was that she had been told that she should be negotiating with HR and no one else.

The manager at the company shook his head. "I could have done something about that," he told her.

As a general rule, talk to the people who are the most invested in having you join them. In fairness, it should be noted that sometimes HR has more knowledge and experience than line managers and also understands where there is flexibility, including what can be done to improve compensation packages—even more than line managers do. You need to use judgment regarding whom you talk to and why.

Say that you want the job.

In the interview process be enthusiastic. If you want the job, let them know. Enthusiasm breeds generosity in the salary negotiation process. Nobody, however, wants apathy or desperation. (It's like receiving a marriage proposal and saying, "Well, I guess so; it's the best offer I've received in a long time.") Your enthusiasm about the job will also help others connect with you, allowing you to establish rapport and relationship even before you've been hired.

Your Six-Figure Salary Negotiation

The tips about handling negotiations (and there have been entire books written on them) are only that—advice and guidance to help you during the process. What's most important, however, is the content and framework for finding the right job, with the compensation, opportunity, challenge, people, and culture to provide you with maximum career satisfaction and enjoyment of life.

Job satisfaction is the result of full engagement with challenging, meaningful objectives, working with people aligned with purpose and mission, who are engaged together toward common ends. If you're working for the right organization, doing the right job—asking questions, contributing as much as you can, and learning and growing—your compensation will follow. Ideally, the negotiation process will set up rules and the framework within which you will succeed and contribute.

My goal in writing this book is to provide you with expertise and advice from CEOs who shared from their own experience as professionals and as employers. This was my job—my contribution—as I wrote this book. Now it's up to you to find the job that will allow you to maximize your contribution and the value you bring, so that you will be well satisfied and rewarded.

Keep in mind—just as Bob Wright pointed out in Chapter 10— that when you are in the middle of the negotiation process and you start wanting that job, everything goes out the window. Knowing that ahead of time, you can be better prepared, mentally and strategically. The purpose of this book is to remind you of the important points, some of which may seem obvious, but in the midst of interviewing and negotiating are easy to forget.

Just think of the experiences of Dave Jensen (who is a real person, by the way, whose name has been changed). Smart, accomplished, with an impressive resume, as soon as he got into negotiations for his job, he overlooked or didn't feel confident enough to pursue several points, from getting a tour of the office to what some of the next logical career moves would be from that position.

How can you keep from making the same mistakes that Dave did? Get the support you need. As Bob Wright pointed out, having a group of advisors will help you to undertake the necessary due diligence about potential jobs, ask the right questions, and present yourself in the best possible light, so that you can make one of the most important decisions for yourself—choosing the next right job.

Resources

Actuary.org—Offers information related to benefits, as well as a link to the American Academic of Actuaries' Pension Assistance List (PAL) program for people who have questions about their pension plans.

JobStar.org—Provides a variety of information related to job search, as well as links to numerous free salary surveys.

Monster.com—Job posting site with tips for looking for a job, salary negotiation advice, and related information.

Salary.com—Offers salary and compensation tools for professionals, as well as free "Salary Wizard" to benchmark salary for specific job titles in geographic areas (based on zip code).

SalaryExpert.com—Career and compensation advice, including executive compensation reports and global salary calculator, available for a fee.

WetFeet.com—Career advice with free online information such as Q&A interviews with recruiters, advice on creating an effective resume, and salary tools.

Index

Salary (income). *See also* Value
asking for more than offered, 2–3, 77
asking for right amount, 73–74
assessing validity of offer limits,
17–18
contribution, value and, xvii, 31–32,
36–37, 38–39, 42–43, 194, 228,
230. *See also* Performance
cuts, 35
exceeding range, 83–84, 101
fixating on, and overlooking job fit,
13–14
getting advice in negotiating, 19
growth potential, 32–34
happiness and, 32–36, 40, 42, 159
increases, 80–85. *See also*
Negotiating with current employer
market for. *See* Market, knowing
money generators and, 93–94
as primary motivator, 113–15
ranges, knowing, 74–80, 94–95, 226,
229
real negotiation issues and, 14–16
relative importance of, 40
self-worth and, 9–10, 209, 211–12,
215
stock options and, 89–93
Sales process, 203–23
Bob Wright on, 205–21
buyer mentality, 203–5, 207, 211,
213, 220, 228
buyer-type questions, 218–19, 223
car buying/selling metaphor, 212–13
false-buyers, 219–20
fear factor, 206–8, 209
knowing your own personal traps,
216–17
overselling yourself, 194–96
packaging yourself, 170–71, 177
pursuing multiple opportunities,
212–13
self-knowledge and, 214–15
seller mentality, 203–5, 208, 211,
212, 213, 217–18, 228

selling your features and benefits,
98, 228
shifting from buyer to seller, 213–14
vulnerability in, 169–70
Self-reflection
assessment exercise, 20–21
identifying what you value, 25–27, 28
importance of self-knowledge,
66–67, 214–15
Self-worth, 9–10, 209, 211–12, 215
Smith, Stan, on value, 24–44
Stock options, 89–93

Terry, Tom, 120–21. *See also* Benefit
package
Trust, 191–92, 227

Value, 23–45. *See also* Performance;
Salary (income)
assessment exercise, 45
of challenge, 31–32, 35–36, 42–43
common drivers of, 27–29
to company, 36–39
components of, 25
of contribution, xvii, 31–32, 36–37,
38–39, 42–43
of diverse experiences, 41–42
identifying what you value, 25–28
life stage impacting, 41–44
of other non-monetary things,
29–30, 229
perspective on, 23–24, 44
of proper job fit, xv, 13–14, 25–27,
28, 231
of recognition, 37, 229
of security, 41
Stan Smith on, 25–44
of time, 39–41

Wellness programs, 130–31
White, William, 180. *See also* Employer
perspective
Women, 139–62
asking for feedback in interviews,
153–54, 155